The virgin of th

A play, in five acts

August von Kotzebue

(Translator: Anne Plumptre)

Alpha Editions

This edition published in 2024

ISBN : 9789362998163

Design and Setting By
Alpha Editions
www.alphaedis.com
Email - info@alphaedis.com

Contents

THE
AUTHOR's DEDICATION.

TO MADAME VON DER WENSE, OF THE FAMILY OF AHLEFELD
AT ZELL, LADY OF THE PRESIDENT VON DER WENSE.

It has frequently been said, that poetry, like love, cannot be commanded. This, my very amiable Friend must now acknowledge to be an error, since, if her memory be accurate with regard to trifles, she will recollect, that this Drama owes its origin solely and entirely to her commands.

One evening at Pyrmont, the weather being too wet and melancholy to permit of her enjoying the charms of nature, to which her pure soul is so closely allied, she had recourse to the Temple of Thalia, where Naumann's Opera of Cora happened to be represented. The performers were of a very inferior kind, and the only thing that pleased me during the evening, was that I had the good fortune to sit behind my Friend, who sometimes condescended to favour her humble servant with a little conversation. Among other remarks which the occasion called forth, she observed once, when the conclusion of an act gave us a short respite from being merely auditors, that the Opera at which we were present, contained excellent ground work for a Drama.

I felt that this idea ought rather to have originated with me, but I easily found an excuse for my apparent negligence, in the circumstance of my being in company with one whose powers of pleasing were so great and so various, as to preclude, wherever she was present, the intervention of any other thoughts but what her own perfections inspired. Yet I caught eagerly at the idea when once suggested, and declared to my friend that her commands only were requisite for the immediate employment of my pen upon the subject. For a long time she evaded honouring me with such a command, preferring, in all that she said to encourage me to the undertaking, the politer language of exhortation, to which her gentle nature is more accustomed. I however insisted upon a positive command.

"*Well then, I command it,*" she said, at last, with the naïveté so peculiarly her own.—I made a low bow, and now have the honour of presenting to her my VIRGIN OF THE SUN. At her command the trembling maiden appears with downcast eyes in the anti-chamber, and hopes for permission humbly to wait there, till a friendly invitation shall call her to the toilette of her Patroness.

"Come nearer, gentle creature!—thou shalt be welcome to me for the sake of thy father, with whom I have long lived on terms of friendship, and whom

I should now be the more scrupulous of depriving of what does remain to him, since he has so little that is desirable left in the world."

Ah, you are but too much in the right, my most amiable friend!—I once possessed a treasure who greatly resembled you, inasmuch as she was one of the best of wives, and of mothers. But she is gone to her proper home, to the society of angels. At the moment when I experienced this most severe of all afflictions, you benignantly embalmed my sorrows with a tear;—for that tear my heart retains a lasting gratitude, and my pen gladly embraces an opportunity, at the same time of dedicating my work to you, and of giving this public testimony of the high esteem entertained for you, by

AUGUSTUS VON KOTZEBUE.

DRAMATIS PERSONÆ.

ATALIBA, *King of Quito.*

The HIGH-PRIEST *of the* SUN.

XAIRA, *another Priest of the* SUN.

TELASCO, *an Old Man of the Family of the* INCAS.

ZORAI, *his Son.*

CORA, *his Daughter, the* VIRGIN OF THE SUN.

ROLLA, *formerly General of the Peruvian Army.*

The HIGH-PRIESTESS *of the* SUN.

IDALI,   }   VIRGINS OF THE SUN.

AMAZILI,   }

DON ALONZO MOLINA, *a Spaniard.*

DON JUAN VELASQUEZ, *his Friend.*

DIEGO, *an Attendant on* DON ALONZO.

A CHAMBERLAIN *to the King.*

PRIESTS OF THE SUN, VIRGINS OF THE SUN, COURTIERS, SOLDIERS, POPULACE.

ACT I.

SCENE I.—*A wild and woody Country, where the Bushes and Underwood are so closely entwined as to be almost impenetrable. In the Back-ground, a Wall, in which a large Breach has been made, is just discernible through the Trees; and farther back, rises the Cupola of the Temple of the Sun. Nearer the Front, on the right Hand, appears a Cave; on the left, a Hill, the Top of which is seen above the Trees.*

ROLLA *comes down a winding Path among the Bushes, followed by the* HIGH-PRIEST.

HIGH-PRIEST.

And this is the way to Rolla's dwelling?—Ah, equally wild and inaccessible as the way to Rolla's heart!

Rolla. Spare me, uncle, I entreat you?—spare me, and leave me!—If you could understand me——

High-Priest. Ought I to attempt it?—To understand thee, means to pay homage to thy idol,—to flatter thy passion.

Rolla. Unhappy wretch that I am!—I am a miserable solitary being!—a drop, which can find no kindred drop wherewith to associate!—a lonely voice, which cannot find its echo throughout all animated nature. The worm that crawls upon this leaf soon meets its help-mate, with whom it is united—but I—I alone!—Oh ye gods! if it be your harsh will that, amid the throne of living creatures which animate creation, I only should be left alone!—(*casting an impatient glance upon the High-Priest*) Then—man!—man!—leave me alone!

High-Priest. Rolla! Rolla! I am indeed old, yet if affection only be wanting to bring repose to thy heart, thou wilt find it here in this faithful bosom.—Young man, I love thee as a father.

Rolla. Well then, if the happiness of thy son be dear to thee, suffer him to live according to his own pleasure!—In this cave I am far happier than thousands who inhabit pompous palaces. Be this my grave!—only make me this promise, uncle; it is my sole request: When I shall be no more, then, on some dark melancholy day, lead Cora to the entrance of my rugged habitation, and shew her the remains of Rolla, as they lie upon the cold damp earth on which he breathed out a life that love had rendered miserable. Let her see those lips on which the name of his beloved murderer quivered even to the last gasp; and by the smile still resting on them, let her know that they closed blessing the name of Cora. Then perhaps, affected by this picture, she may strew flowers over my corpse; or—oh transporting thought!—even embalm it with a tear!—A tear!—ah! a tear from Cora would recall it again to life.

High-Priest. Oh enthusiast!

Rolla. Call me what you please!—Yet, if I be an enthusiast, think not that I am suddenly become so. This heart was born to be the seat of mighty passions.—To the common swarm of emmets which bustle about the world, I had an aversion, even as a boy. When my play-mates were merry and sportive around me, I played it is true, but I always found it irksome, though I never could precisely ascertain to what cause that feeling might be ascribed. But when storms lowered around the horizon, when our mountains vomited forth flames at midnight, or subterraneous groanings announced an approaching earthquake, then my heart felt elevated; my languishing spirit revived; the withered plant again reared its head. As I advanced in life, no female attractions had power to charm my eyes;—they remained stedfastly and eagerly fixed on the more brilliant rays of honour. Blinded to every beauty of nature, my heart, my throbbing heart, burned solely to run the career of fame and glory; while each victory that I obtained, far from proving an assuaging drop to mitigate the flame, served only to encrease its ardour.— Then it was that I saw Cora again!

High-Priest. And the flame which at first burst out with a force that promised its eternal duration, was instantly extinguished!—Extinguished as a lamp by the breath of a child.

Rolla. No, not so!—The flame continued to burn, it only found a different species of nourishment. What was before a wild and all-consuming blaze, was changed into a gentle, genial warmth. Honour gave way to love.

High-Priest. A gentle, genial warmth!—these words sound well, indeed—But whom does thy flame illumine?—whom does it warm?

Rolla. (*With indifference*) I feel what you would say.

High-Priest. You feel it, yet are not ashamed?—Young man!—endowed with powers to achieve the noblest deeds, perhaps to form the blessing of a whole hemisphere, you contract your circle of action—within a CAVE!—Inca, born of the race of the children of the sun, entitled to become one of the first bulwarks of the throne, you fly—into a CAVE!—Leader; entrusted by your native country with the conduct of her armies, and thus called upon, by a succession of noble actions, to prove yourself worthy so honourable a confidence, you can yet bury yourself—in a CAVE!—

Rolla. Would you seduce me to be a boaster?—As Inca, and as leader of the armies of my country, I have fulfilled my duty through wounds and victories!—Have I not at various times proved myself deserving of her confidence!—Was not this more particularly proved on that awful day when

Ataliba's throne was shaken by Huascar's power, and Rolla's sword dyed the fields of Tumibamba with the blood of his sovereign's enemies. Know you not the history of that day?—One arrow was lodged in my left arm, another pierced my breast; I received a large gash in my cheek from a sword, and was stunned by the stroke of a club upon my forehead. Look at the scars of those wounds, here, and here, and here!—Yet I never stirred from the field of battle.—Tell me now, have I given my country cause to repent her confidence?

High-Priest. (*Much affected*) Brave youth!—But were the blessings of thy native-country, the friendship of thy sovereign, and the love and shouts of thy army, no recompense to thy heart?

Rolla. (*With a sigh*) They were!

High-Priest. But are so no longer?

Rolla. No!

High-Priest. Oh ye gods! 'tis thus by annihilating the former man, that you chastise this unworthy love which blights every noble germ implanted in the heart!

Rolla. Judge not so harshly!—Love, like honour, is the parent of great actions!—But I—for whom should I fight?—Is there on earth a heart to which I should communicate joy, were I longer to pursue the road to fame?—Cora does not love me!—I have neither father nor mother, neither brother nor sister!—I am alone in the world.

High-Priest. (*Clasping him in his arms*) My son!—my son!

Rolla. Leave me, leave me, uncle!—I cannot return this love. You, with those grey hairs, clothed in those priestly garments, bearing an appearance so solemn, so entitled to respect, can never become the confident of my bosom. In you I cannot separate the man from the dignity of the priesthood.—Ah that I had a mother!—God created woman to be the confident of man!—Canst thou not share thy sorrows with her who loves thee? then fly to thy mother!—But I—I enjoy not the love of any one!—I have no mother!

High-Priest. Fly then to the gods!

Rolla. The gods hate me, because I love a maiden who is devoted to their service—because I love this maiden more than I love the gods themselves?—Whether I behold the sun rise, or see Cora appear, a like impression is made upon my senses, upon my heart!—Ah no!—Cora makes the strongest impression on both.

High-Priest. May the gods pardon this enthusiasm!—Ah, Rolla! it is thus that the children of mortality always desire most eagerly, what is impossible to be attained. Cora, the maiden, had only pleased your fancy—Cora, the Virgin of the Sun, you love with unbounded passion.

Rolla. (*With rising warmth*) What!—(*he restrains himself; but casts a look of indignation upon the High-Priest*) Good night, uncle. (*He is going into his cave.*)

High-Priest. Whither art thou going, young man?—Cannot thy friend, thy sincere friend, obtain some little influence over thee?—Live according to thy own pleasure!—Withdraw thyself if thou wilt from mankind, only fly this desert, where fatal images inevitably disturb thy soul, as the wild thorns thy senses. Come to my house!—that quarter of it which runs down to the sea shore is well known to thee;—there may'st thou live sequestered and in solitude, even in the midst of thousands; and there no importunate intruder shall deprive thee of the visions which thy heart so fondly loves to cherish. Thy doors may be closed against me—mine shall always be open to thee.

Rolla. Uncle, accept my thanks. I feel these proposals to be meant in kindness—I know your habitation; I know that it abounds with charms for those who love retirement; but Rolla is resolved to live and die in this cave. There, where the cupola of the temple towers above the trees—there Cora lives—here I can at least behold her dwelling.—Rolla, then, must live and die in this cave!—Good night.

High-Priest. Obstinate young man!—Yet, surely you will not forget what your duty requires during the solemnities of to-morrow. Your presence in the king's palace, and in the temple, is indispensible at the grand festival of the Sun.

Rolla. Excuse me!—Say what you please to the king—tell him I am dead—I come no more among men. Yet to-morrow I will sacrifice to the gods—whether in a temple, or in a cave, is alike acceptable to them.—Good night. [*Exit into his cave.*

SCENE II.—*The* HIGH-PRIEST *alone.*

Young man!—young man!—thou dost not suspect how deeply this heart is interested in thy repose!—But the evening sun already glitters upon the golden cupola of the temple, and here below amid these trees, the night is fast approaching. I fear I shall find some difficulty in tracing out the meandering path through this wilderness. (*As he is going, he almost runs against Diego.*)

SCENE III.—DIEGO *gropes his Way through the Bushes, and starts violently at meeting the* HIGH-PRIEST.

High-Priest. Whence come you?—and whither would you go?

Diego. Whithersoever chance may conduct a pedestrian.

High-Priest. Do you walk for pleasure in such unbeaten ways?

Diego. (*Pertly*) Yes.

High-Priest. You may probably have mistaken your path?

Diego. So it should seem, since I find myself in your way.

High-Priest. Are you not Don Alonzo's attendant?

Diego. You are not very wide of the truth.

High-Priest. If you be not well acquainted with this wood, you are in great danger of losing yourself. Accompany me, and I will conduct you in a short time into the right path.

Diego. (*Assuming an angry tone*) Who told you that I was in the wrong path?—Signor High-Priest, I would have you to know, that neither in Castile nor Arragon, neither in Grenada nor Murcia, no, nor in any other of the countries belonging to my king, by whatsoever name distinguished, has any mother's son ever been known to excel Diego in valour and virtue.

High-Priest. (*smiling*) I readily believe it. And what gives the greater currency to this assurance is, that it is uttered by yourself.

Diego. It was forcibly extorted by you, from my modesty.

High-Priest. Pardon me!—And now permit me to request an explanation of this riddle?—How can you be wandering at night in so wild a spot as this, and yet be in the right way?—Are you alone, or is your master near?—What is it you want?—for never can I be persuaded that you come hither only for a walk.

Diego. (*with hesitation*) Since you press me so closely then—I—must confess—that—I am in love.

High-Priest. (*smiling*) You are in love?

Diego. (*extravagantly*) Yes, in love to desperation!—I am tortured with jealousy; driven almost to phrenzy!—In the tumult of passion I am now hurried up to the summits of the highest hills, now driven into the lowest recesses of a subterranean cavern,—till at length I have wandered insensibly into this spot, devoted to tender feelings, here to hold solitary intercourse with the mournful turtle-doves.

High-Priest. This spot does indeed seem to be selected by the gods, as an asylum for enamoured fools.

Diego. Here will I tell of my sorrows to the silent trees!—here breathe out my amorous sighs to the chaste moon!

High-Priest. Thou art a coxcomb! (*Exit.*)

Diego. (*Alone*) A coxcomb!—So much the worse for you Signor!—for if such be the case, the most illustrious High-Priest of the Sun has been made the sport of a coxcomb. Live wit, say I—it will fetch its price in the new world, as well as in the old.—But is he really gone?—Yes.—I hear nothing more!— Hist!—Hist!—(*He goes and looks out at the other side of the stage.*)

SCENE IV.—*Enter* DON ALONZO *and* DON JUAN. *The latter with a large Cloak wrapped round him.*

Juan. Are we safe, Diego?

Diego. A fine question, truly.—Yes, as safe as men can be who are wandering about a forest in the dead of night, and under the open canopy of heaven, after, saving your honour's presence, a piece of knavery. By Saint Barnabas I believe we are about as safe as a drunkard who should attempt to cross the river Amazons upon a wire.

Juan. Have you seen any thing?

Diego. In the dark I seldom *see* any thing—but I have *heard*—

Alonzo. What!—what have you heard?

Diego. The voice of the great High-Priest himself.

Alonzo. The High-Priest!—What could he want here?

Diego. To put me into the right path, nothing more. It is the same in this, as in all other countries, Priests are the only people who are able to lead us into the right path.

Alonzo. But what could bring him into this wilderness?—Oh, speak, Velasquez!—tell me, what dost thou think could be his errand?

Juan. To what purpose speak? What end can conjecture serve? To rush with my sword drawn, and eyes averted, into the thickest of the press, is my maxim in any case of danger. Talking dissipates courage, as a shower disperses the thin coat of earth scattered over a rock, so that no foundation remains from which any adventurous action can shoot forth. If I were disposed to talk, I could find enough to say.

Alonzo. Of what nature?

Diego. Oh speak, Sir, I entreat you!—When it is dark I always like to hear talking.

Juan. Well, it shall be so. It may amuse you too, Alonzo, till the hour when your constellation shall rise; for the time always appears horribly tedious when one is waiting for a tender appointment. I will therefore talk till you command my silence; and this shall be the text with which I introduce my discourse.—My friend, this adventure bodes no good!—believe me, it bodes no good!

Diego. Right, Sir, right.

Alonzo. This is language foreign to thy sentiments. When has the time been known that Don Juan Velasquez turned his back upon an adventure, because it was dangerous?

Juan. There is the matter!—Hear me, Alonzo!—If thou wert capable of doubting my courage, I might easily prove it, by engaging the next rattle-snake I should meet. Thou knowest my principle, that I do not value my life more highly, than a moment of happiness, and happy is every moment that I sacrifice to friendship. If, therefore, thou hast any regard for me, no more of this!—My arm, my sword, are devoted to thy service—I have followed thee blindly into the labyrinth in which we are now involved; but I must still be permitted to think, that we do not give any proof of our wisdom in groping our way here when we might be more advantageously employed.

Alonzo. More advantageously?—let me hear in what way?

Juan. He who is doing ill, may always be more advantageously employed; and by the blood of all the knights that does or does not flow in my veins, I think we are now cursedly in the wrong. I say nothing of the sword suspended by a thread over our heads—affection takes precedence of life—You love Cora—I have the strongest attachment to you, and Diego is attached to both.

Diego. Certainly, certainly, Sir!—but—notwithstanding—pray don't take it amiss, if I think that life has precedence of affection.

Juan. Granted therefore that the prosecution of this enterprise should prove the means of shortening the duration of our lives, yet we perhaps only give up some years of unhappiness ourselves, to purchase the happiness of a friend.—And since they have lived long, who have lived happily, and he only can be esteemed to have lived happily who has died so; what better can we wish, or how can we end our lives more satisfactorily, than in offering them up a sacrifice to friendship.

Diego. Cursed maxims, these!

Juan. But, Alonzo, to be happy, according to my ideas of happiness, you will understand that I consider this salutary state of the soul as inseparable from integrity and virtue. Lay your hand then upon your heart, and tell me what are now your feelings in moments of temperance and reflection?—Don Alonzo Molina quitted the savage followers of Pizarro, because he abhorred their barbarities—that was a noble principle!—I will go, he said, among these mild and benevolent people, and by cultivating their minds, and instructing them in the arts of civilized life, become their friend and benefactor.— Objects worthy of my friend!—But what has been the end of these virtuous resolutions?—You came among them indeed—the king of the country received you with open arms and an expanded heart—the people loved you—the family of the Incas honoured you—the great men of the nation beheld you without envy, enjoying the favour of their sovereign. You shared that sovereign's cares; but you also shared his joys, his wealth;—you were no longer considered as a foreigner, and even the priests themselves murmured not when they saw you appear at the worship of their gods.—Oh fatal forbearance!—On one of these solemn days, my noble friend beheld in the temple one of the priestesses of the sun, as she presented the bread of sacrifice to the king.—She was young—she was lovely—Alonzo's heart was instantly lost—and at the same moment all the grand designs he had formed, were sunk in the ocean of forgetfulness.—The champion for the rights of humanity slumbered upon his post, while the charming device upon his shield, the united hands beneath a cross surrounded with sun-beams, gave way to a burning heart, pierced through with arrows.—And now, if I wish to speak with Alonzo, where must I seek him?—Among the counsellors of the king—the judges of the people—or the instructors of youth?—It was among these, or such as these, that I should once have expected to find him:—but now, now he is only to be found stealing nightly about these walls, or behind these walls, with his face deeply buried in his cloak, hiding himself from his own conscience—while all his glorious projects are crushed in the embryo, as the future brood is destroyed by a mischievous boy who breaks the eggs of the setting hen.

Alonzo. (Indignantly) Velasquez!

Juan. Away with that menacing countenance, it ill accords with your situation. A man should not dare to assume the privilege of growing angry, unless his conscience be pure.—You will perhaps wonder at the jocund Velasquez becoming on a sudden a preacher of morality—but Velasquez was only jocund and light-hearted, because he was an honest man—let him therefore preach on, since he has entered upon the subject. You, by whom formerly every article of popular faith, even to the most minute, was held inviolate, because you considered that to every one was attached, in a considerable degree, the peace of mind of some weak, but honest man—you now rashly bid defiance to one of the most sacred tenets of a whole nation that has received you hospitably into their bosom, and seduce a chaste virgin devoted to their gods.—The conflicts of nature herself, are made subservient to your desires; and while a dreadful earthquake shakes these inaccessible walls even to their foundation, the bold intruder takes advantage of the passage thus opened to him to rush into Cora's arms, and amidst this elemental warfare to murder innocence.

Alonzo. Forbear, Velasquez!—have you no compassion for me?—believe me, my conscience does not slumber.

Juan. Well then, if it slumber not, it is at least deaf, and the malady must be removed.—Ataliba is thy benefactor,—this amiable people have received thee as a brother,—and thou, assassin-like, art stabbing them in the dark.

Alonzo. Oh Velasquez, once more I entreat you to forbear!—I acknowledge, with gratitude, the voice of friendship,—but what wouldst thou require of me?

Juan. Heaven be thanked that I have succeeded at last in awakening you to some degree of reflection!—I require of you instantly to renounce this dangerous and criminal intercourse.

Alonzo. Well, I will consult with Cora.

Juan. Most admirable!—Cora is indeed the proper person to decide upon this matter. I perceive that you are seriously impressed with my lecture.

Alonzo. Rely upon me!—I will represent to her all that anxious love can suggest—the anger of the king—the indignation of the people—my danger—

Juan. Your danger!—Pardon the interruption, my friend, but you speak here without much reflection!—Your danger put in the balance against hers, is as a handful of down weighed against a bar of gold. You hazard only your life—

Diego. What the devil, and is not that enough?

Juan. She, on the contrary, hazards her fame, her repose, her father's blessing, the love of her family, her prospect of salvation—and, to sum up all—she must encounter the most horrible of all deaths, supposing that this intercourse should give existence to a being who would prove the betrayer of your loves.

Alonzo. Oh talk not of it!—No, no, Velasquez, thank heaven I am not so deeply involved in guilt!

Juan. Heaven be thanked indeed, if you are yet clear from it?—but while you continue in your present course, what security can you have, that you will always remain so. And should a consequence so fatal ensue, think only on the boundless misery that it must bring both on Cora and yourself. That she must die would be little; the horrible idea is, the manner of her death. Shut up alive in a subterraneous vault, the opening of which will be closed upon her for ever, with only a single loaf of bread and a small lamp, she must sit gasping for air, and soon endure the severest torments of hunger.—Oh the very thought makes me shudder!—I have encountered death undauntedly under a variety of forms; but I could not bear to meet him under this.

Alonzo. (*Falling on his neck.*) I will never see Cora again!

Juan. Worthily resolved!—let us then instantly depart!—(*Endeavours to draw him away.*)

Alonzo. Only permit me to take leave of her!

Juan. Write her a letter, which we will throw over the wall—You hesitate!—Oh you are undecided!—Ha! already I see the hapless Cora enclosed in her horrible dungeon, crushed by the two-fold agony of bodily and mental torments, lying on the ground and gnawing her own flesh—uttering the most dreadful execrations against her God, and amid the wildest ravings of phrenzy breathing out that soul, the purity of which was poisoned by thee. Then when she shall stand before him who hereafter will judge alike the Peruvian and the Spaniard, and shall accuse thee as the origin of all her woes, the occasion of her becoming the murderer of her child——

Alonzo. (*Eagerly pulling Juan forwards.*) Come, come!—let us fly!

Juan. With the utmost transport! (*As they are going, a clapping of hands is heard behind the wall.*)

Alonzo. (*Turning suddenly round*) That is her signal! my Cora! my Cora!—(*He breaks away from Velasquez, and climbs hastily over the breach in the wall.*)

SCENE V.—DON JUAN, *and* DIEGO. *Juan looks after Alonzo with Astonishment and Indignation.*

Diego. (*After a pause.*) Now do I defy any one to assert again, that sound is an empty thing—a nothing. The most reverend Don Juan Velasquez has been for a long time holding such a discourse here as is not delivered every day, even from the pulpit of Salamanca, but the moment that three or four claps are given by a pair of heathenish hands, the wretch for whose benefit this fine oration was intended, loses every beneficial impression, gives them all to the winds, and runs headlong after his own wild inventions.

Juan. (*With some asperity*) Farewell my friend! Since thou art resolved on ruin, take thine own course!—Oh madman! madman!—where others only walk he runs, where others enter slowly and only step by step, thither he rushes. Well, well, even if what I have urged prove of no avail, friendship has however discharged its duty—and the worst that can happen is at last to be reduced to suffer with my friend. Till then, be of good heart, Diego!—How dost thou find thyself?

Diego. Like a fish upon dry land.

Juan. Thou dost not speak truly. When a fool is running on the wrong side of the post, he is in his proper element; and, by Saint George, I think we are running cursedly on the wrong side of the post here.

Diego. Only with this difference, that I *must* do as you *please*—and you are not *pleased* to do what God and sound reason require of you.

Juan. Well, let us hear what your wisdom would suggest.

Diego. Were I in the place of the valiant knight Don Juan de Velasquez, in the first place I would deliver a discourse pretty nearly to the same purpose as he has done; but then if that produced no effect, I would say—my dear friend Alonzo, or my dear Don Alonzo, you cannot expect that I should stay to be roasted alive for your sake!—Fare thee well—I shall return home, and take our worthy Diego with me.—We will say over our beads in your behalf.

Juan. That may as well be done here.

Diego. Here!—on heathen ground!—in view of a heathen temple!

Juan. Blockhead!—Our God is every where, and by a firm adherence to the sacred claims of friendship we serve him more acceptably than by saying over a rosary—therefore will I offer no prayers at this moment. I am here as the guardian of my misguided friend.

Diego. And pray then in what capacity am I here?

Juan. As his attendant, whom he employs to carry his arms.

Diego. My presence then, it should seem, is now wholly superfluous, since I am not permitted to appear publickly as such.

Juan. Thy part is to obey, not to remonstrate. Go, take this whistle, and steal silently to the left, along the wall that surrounds the Temple, while I go round by the right—we shall by this means meet on the other side; and should you encounter any thing suspicious by the way, make use of the whistle. Here, take it.

Diego. (*Trembling as he takes it*) To the left did you say?

Juan. Yes, to the left.

Diego. And quite alone?

Juan. Yes, quite alone.

Diego. I am afraid of losing myself among the bushes.

Juan. Fool, can you not see the wall, and the cupola of the Temple?

Diego. Do you take me for an owl?

Juan. Is not the moon bright enough to light thee?

Diego. No.

Juan. No!—Ha! ha! ha!—Fear seems wholly to have deprived Signor Diego of his senses.

Diego. I must beg leave to observe, Sir, that the night is devoted to rest, and even if the man himself be not allowed to sleep, his internal courage, commonly takes the liberty of enjoying a comfortable nap. My fortitude always goes to bed with the sun.

Juan. (*Going up to him earnestly*) Friend Diego, we will awaken it with some hearty blows.

Diego. (*Shrinking away from him*) Oh it is easily awakened: it does not sleep very soundly.

Juan. Go, then, fool!—(*He thrusts him off on one side. and goes off himself on the other.*)

SCENE VI.—ALONZO *springs over the Ruins of the Wall, and then reaches his Hand to* CORA, *who follows him.*

Alonzo. (*As he assists her*) Only one little jump, dear Cora!—throw yourself boldly into my arms!—Here will you find a secret and retired spot, formed for love, and guarded by friends. This is not so wide and waste a scene as your garden, in which, barren as it is of all shade, the treacherous moon betrays every form that ventures within its circuit. (*He presses her to his bosom*) At length I have thee in my arms again.

Cora. (*Returning his embrace*) And I have thee again in mine.

Alonzo. Ah! it is now three long weeks——

Cora. Only three weeks?

Alonzo. Months to love.

Cora. Years to my heart.

Alonzo. Every evening at twilight has poor Alonzo wandered hither, and listened in anxious expectation of the signal which might summon him to a night of transport.

Cora. And every evening has Cora wept because she dared not meet Alonzo.

Alonzo. You have not been ill, I hope.

Cora. Ah! I am always ill when I am not with you.

Alonzo. Say, dearest Cora, what has prevented our meeting?—You promised that I should sooner——

Cora. Did I *promise?*—That was not right, as I could only hope that it might be sooner; but love always adds hopes to its wishes, and too soon begins to consider those hopes as certainties. It does not often fall to my lot to take the nightly service in the temple, but I relied upon having the turn of one of my companions who was ill, and whose place I had offered to supply. She, however, recovered; and, instead of the promised happiness, I had only her thanks for my intentions. Poor Cora was heartily vexed at this disappointment, and her sleepless nights appeared so tedious.

Alonzo. Alas! I have also been a stranger to rest. The dews of morning found me under these trees, while my cloaths were still damp with the dews of the past evening, and my limbs still shivered with the cold of midnight. Beneath yon palm-tree have I stood, night after night, with my eyes fixed upon your temple; and often, as I have seen a form wander backwards and forwards, where glimmers the eternal lamp, I have pleased myself with thinking that it might be Cora's.

Cora. It was not that in my solitude I could be deceived by shadows, yet I seemed every where to see your image. The idea made me restless, and I ran with hurried steps hither and thither—kept incessantly moving from one spot to another. Oh tell me, does love always render people impatient?—It was not thus with me formerly; but I was gentle, quiet, and bore without a murmur the failure of any trifling wish; the disappointment of any cherished expectation—whether it were that a shower deprived me of a promised walk, or that the wind destroyed the flowers which I had carefully reared with my own hands. Now all is changed; I am no longer the same person. When I sit at my daily employments, and spin, or weave, if a thread happen to break, I am so peevish that I sometimes even startle at myself. (*Caressing him*) Tell me, Alonzo, does love improve, or spoil us?

Alonzo. True love improves.

Cora. Oh no, no!—True love reigns in my heart, yet I am not so good as I was.

Alonzo. It is only that thy blood runs somewhat more swiftly.

Cora. Or else that I am ill.—Yes, I am now often ill.

Alonzo. Indeed!

Cora. Yes, indeed!—But that must be so—for soon—soon—I shall not love you alone.

Alonzo. (*Starting*) Not me alone?

Cora. (*Smiling*) Not you alone!

Alonzo. Your words involve a riddle, or else a crime. Cora, love cannot comprehend more than one object.—You will not love me alone? (*He fixes his eyes earnestly upon her*) No, you cannot mean to say so—if it were true, you could not look at me with so much composure, such perfect unreserve.

Cora. And why should I not look at you with composure?—My feelings are so sweet that they cannot be criminal. An unknown, but pleasing sadness has taken possession of my heart—I experience sensations not to be described. When lately at the Solstitial feast, I was ornamenting the porch of the temple with flowers, I saw upon the lowest of the steps which lead up to it, a young woman sleeping, at whose breast lay a little smiling angel: my heart was altogether dissolved at so interesting a spectacle, and I involuntarily stretched out my arms to the child, intending to take it gently from its mother, and press it to my bosom. But how easily are the slumbers of a tender mother disturbed; for scarcely had I touched the babe ere she awoke, rose up anxiously, clasped her treasure to her heart, and cast on me a look of deep distrust. Say, Alonzo?—Do you not think an affectionate mother one of the most respectable of creatures?

Alonzo. (*Bewildered*) Oh, why that question?

Cora. Can't you guess?—(*With pure and innocent transport*) I shall soon be a mother myself.

Alonzo. (*Thunderstruck*) Great God!!!

Cora. What is the matter?—You need not be alarmed!—I love you more than ever!—Ah, at the first commencement of our love I thought it impossible that the attachment I then felt could ever be exceeded; for in you, Alonzo, I beheld the most charming of youths. But, enchanter, you have stolen into my heart under a still more attractive form, since I behold in you, the father of my child.

Alonzo. Cora! Cora!—my hair is erect with horror, while your mind seems wholly at ease.

Cora. And what do you fear?—Is it a crime to become a mother?—My father always taught me, that whoever commits a crime, instantly forfeits all peace of mind; but for me, I feel no uneasiness.

Alonzo. Do you not recollect the circumstances of your situation?—To what rigid ordinances you swore obedience when this figure of the sun was fastened upon your bosom?

Cora. I swore to obey the ordinances of our temple.

Alonzo. And what do they enjoin you?

Cora. I know not. My father told me, that by whomsoever virtue was held sacred, its precepts would be fulfilled without particular instruction. To me virtue is sacred.

Alonzo. And know you then what constitutes virtue?—Alas! your uncorrupted soul is ignorant of the terrible distinction between virtue as founded in the eternal principles of nature, and virtue as constituted by the distorted imaginations of fanatics. (*He clasps her eagerly in his arms*) Oh, Cora! Cora! what have we done?—In other situations, love and joy recompense the anguish which every mother must endure—in yours alone, those sufferings, however severe, are but the forerunners of others still more dreadful, in the most horrible of all deaths.

Cora. Death!

Alonzo. (*In accents of despair*) And I—I am your murderer!

Cora. (*With composure*) How can you thus unnecessarily torment yourself?—Wherefore, and by whom, should I be put to death?

Alonzo. The priests will affirm, that you have offended the gods.

Cora. I offended the gods!—No, Alonzo, I love the gods.

Alonzo. Cora, I do not doubt it; yet you must become the victim of an ancient superstition. Our only safety would be in flight; but, alas! whither can we fly in a foreign land?

Cora. Be composed, dear enthusiast!—I have thought of means to console you.

Alonzo. If so, it must be the suggestion of God himself.

Cora. The plan is simple, yet will give me certain assurance whether or not the gods are really incensed against me; and the approaching morning may decide this important question. Hitherto the moon and stars alone have been the confidents of our love; but the sun himself, the greatest of all our gods, shall now be witness to it.—At present I dare not stay any longer, for I must hasten back to attend the eternal lamp in the temple. Do you then, Alonzo, rest here under these trees, and, as soon as the dawn of morning shall begin to gild the eastern horizon, I will return, and we will ascend yonder hill together. Then will we turn our faces towards the east, entwine our arms within each other, join lip to lip, and thus boldly wait the rising of the sun.— You understand me?

Alonzo. But half.

Cora. Do you not comprehend, that if Cora have done evil, either the sun will veil himself from her sight, or the first ray of his light that falls upon her, will annihilate the criminal. But if, oh Alonzo! he, my Father, and my God, shall rise clear and resplendent—if he shall smile upon the affectionate pair as he beholds them joined in mutual embrace, then shall we have a certain token that he favours our love, and your mind may be relieved from its cares—for when satisfied that we are guiltless in the eyes of the sun, whose eyes shall Cora need to fear.

Alonzo. Oh affecting simplicity!—Oh sweetest of thy sex!

Cora. But, more still remains, my Alonzo. To-morrow is the grand festival of the sun—if on that day he rise in unveiled majesty, we always regard it as a joyful signal, that the gods are favourably disposed towards us, consequently that no dreadful crime can have called forth their anger. Then look up, Alonzo; cast thy eyes around the heavens; behold how the stars glitter; how blue and serene is every part within our view!—not a cloud threatens us— not a zephyr moves the trees—Oh we shall have a glorious morning!—One embrace then at parting—farewell!—Let Cora at her return find thee sleeping beneath these trees, and then will she awaken thee with a kiss. (*She hastens back through the breach in the wall.*)

Alonzo. (*Who, sunk in astonishment and horror, has scarcely heard what Cora has been saying*) Sweet, benevolent creature!—Oh I have been a villain, the worst of villains! Let me save her!—save her, if it be possible, before the flame shall burst out over her head!—Ah, it is too late! She is irrecoverably lost, and I can only die with her. (*He leans against a tree with both hands upon his forehead.*)

SCENE VII.—DIEGO *enters from the right side, and seeing* ALONZO, *whistles with all his Strength.*

Alonzo. (*Turning round wildly, and grasping his sword*) What is the matter?

Juan. (*Springing forwards from the left side*) What is the matter?

Diego. Is it you, Don Alonzo?—Why did you not say immediately that it was you?

Juan. (*Clapping Diego upon the shoulder*) My friend, you must take a frightened hare for your device.

Diego. Better than a blind lion. Signor Velasquez, you knights consider it as one of the duties of your order to revile prudence as cowardice, in the same manner as we who cannot write, call all learned men, in derision, feather heroes. Did not you yourself order me to whistle whenever I should encounter any thing suspicious?

Juan. Fool! how long has thy master been an object of suspicion to thee?

Diego. To tell you the truth, Signor Don Juan, some time. Look at him now, how he stands there. (*Pointing to Alonzo, who has resumed his former attitude.*)

Juan. (*Shaking Alonzo*) My dear friend, was the adieu then so very heart-breaking?

Alonzo. (*Falling on his neck*) Ah, Velasquez, thy admonitions came too late!

Juan. Oh God!—What!—is she?——

Alonzo. She is indeed!

Juan. Then may we consider our prospect of seeing the kingdom of heaven as no very distant one.

Alonzo. (*Taking Juan's hand*) Oh do not forsake me, my friend, my companion, my brother in arms!

Juan. (*Shaking his hand ardently*) Alonzo, it is not my practice to call to the boy who is struggling in the water, "*You should not have fallen in:*"—I would rather, if it were possible, draw him out. But, by the powers above, I do not know what is to be done here!—Had we a vessel at our command, or could we procure an enchanter's cloak, which would convey us through the air, then would not I be among the last to recommend flight. But since no such means lie at present within our reach, the course to be pursued is not very obvious. Well, well, Velasquez! arm thyself with courage to meet the worst—wrap thyself up in thy cloak, even to the very teeth, and leave the thunder to rattle, and the lightning to flash quietly around thee.

Alonzo. (*Wringing his hands*) All is lost! No resource, no way of escape left!

Juan. Be not so desponding. All is not lost as long as a man retains his senses. Let us depart, eat, drink, and take our rest;—then, by to-morrow, both mind and body will have acquired new strength, and we shall be better able to consider what is to be done.

Diego. Oh, flower of knighthood!

Alonzo. Stop! she will return soon; she promised me at the dawn of morning——

Juan. So, so!—Well, of all employments under the sun, commend me to that of being confident to a lover! They have no idea that a man can have any human feelings—that he must sleep——

Diego. That he must eat—that he must drink—

Alonzo. Forgive me!

Juan. Yes, yes, I forgive you freely; but you must inscribe this sacrifice deeply in your heart; for, by Heaven! the loss of my night's rest—yet, no, rather than lose it, I will repose under the trees. (*He spreads out his cloak, and lies down upon it*) It is always good to make a virtue of necessity; so, with the sage remark, that weariness is the best of all opiates, I wish you a good night, Alonzo. He who has an unsullied conscience can sleep, even with the trunk of a tree only for his pillow, as soundly as the seven sleepers themselves. (*He closes his eyes.*)

Diego. (*Also spreading himself a bed*) If there should happen to be a rattle-snake or two hereabouts—or, perchance, a tyger as hungry as myself!—Hold! an idea occurs to me. (*He takes out a rosary, which he hangs upon the nearest tree*) Now I think we are safe. (*He lies down*) If I can sleep now, who will say that I am not a master in the trade; for my head is full of thought, my heart full of fear, and my poor stomach quite empty. (*He falls asleep.*)

Alonzo. (*Contemplates both for a while, then exclaims*) Happy men! (*He leans in musing melancholy against a tree.*)

(*The Curtain falls.*)

END OF THE FIRST ACT.

ACT II.

SCENE I.—*The Scene remains the same as at the Close of the first Act.* DON JUAN *and* DIEGO *are still sleeping.*—ALONZO *walks about mournfully among the Trees.*

ALONZO.

Will this night never come to an end?—The stars still twinkle in the heavens, the moon scarcely yet begins to lose her lustre, and a deep and solemn silence reigns around.—More grateful to the sinner's soul are noise and tumult, for they assist to deaden the voice of conscience.—What said the fool Diego lately?—that it is the same with conscience as with the stomach, the moment either compels us to feel its existence, we may be sure it is not in perfect health.—And the fool spoke truly.—Oh my excellent mother! thy golden instructions may one day conduct me into a better world—they have not taught me how to conduct myself in another hemisphere!—Perhaps at this very moment thou art upon thy knees, praying for a blessing upon thy fallen son!—Ah, pray for him! intercede for him!—he needs the intercession of a saint!—But away, away ye gloomy thoughts!—All may yet be well!—Night is followed by twilight—twilight by the first rays of the rising sun!—(*Looking towards the east*) And see there the precursor of returning joy!—Already the east begins to be streaked with purple, and the stars are disappearing.—Hist! I hear the chirping of a distant bird!—the moment draws near which is to bring Cora back to her Alonzo!—while I press her to my bosom, conscience is mute, and I can laugh at danger. I will awaken these sleepers. (*He shakes Diego*) Diego, rise,—it is already day.

Diego. (*Rubbing his eyes*) Hey!—how!—you joke! it is still dark.

Alonzo. No, no, the moon is going down, the stars are vanishing.

Diego. (*Yawning*) Take heed what you are about, or you will soon find that it is dark enough. (*He turns on the other side, mutters some inarticulate words, and falls asleep again.*)

Alonzo. If that fellow have not slept, or eaten his fill, he is like a watch not wound up. (*He shakes Don Juan*) Velasquez, the day begins to break!

Juan. (*Raising himself up, and looking about*) Well!—and what of that?

Alonzo. Will you not rise and enjoy so fine a morning?

Juan. Write an Ode upon the Morning, if it be so very fine; but prithee let me sleep quietly. (*He lies down again.*)

Alonzo. Have you forgotten that we may soon expect Cora?

Juan. That is no concern of mine, she does not come to see me.

Alonzo. And don't you think it worth while to unbar your eyes a few minutes earlier, to see an angel?

Juan. I will dream of her. (*He falls asleep.*)

Alonzo. There they lie and sleep as tho' in mockery of the troubles of my soul. Ah, it is only the unembarrassed mind which can thus recruit itself by inactivity. Yes, I perceive that the more man throws off his rational nature, and assimilates himself with the brute, who looks to sense alone for his enjoyments, the happier is his lot.—Happier?—Most certainly so; in his own eyes, at least, if not in the eyes of wisdom; and what more can be required? (*A clapping of hands is heard behind the walls*) But hark?—she comes!—Oh, all that I have said of sensual delight is false! One moment, when the soul partakes of real transport, outweighs whole hours of mere corporeal pleasure. (*He hastens to meet Cora.*)

SCENE II.—CORA *enters and springs into* ALONZO'S *Arms.*

Cora. Here I am, dearest Alonzo!—But you have deprived Cora of an expected pleasure.—I hoped to have found you buried in sleep—I meant to have concealed myself behind a tree, to have scattered leaves over you, and then reproved you as a sluggard.—Do you not hear me, Alonzo, or are you in a waking dream?—else, when your arm is thrown around my neck, how can you stand with eyes thus fixed, and think of any thing besides your Cora?

Alonzo. Amiable creature! suspect me not unjustly!—Cora alone rules in my heart, as one sun alone rules in the heavens.—Yet I cannot cease to think of the discovery made this night!—My peace! my peace of mind is lost!—Conscience,—a thousand horrible images.—Death in its most hideous form, with cold and outstretched arms, tearing Cora from my heart,—these, these are the ideas which haunt me incessantly.

Cora. (*Laying her hand upon his mouth*) Be silent and trust to the gods!—Look up, the heavens are clear and serene all around us, and my heart is full of transport!—Soon will the sun be risen above the horizon, hasten, hasten to ascend the hill! (*She climbs hastily up the hill, Alonzo following her*) Oh behold!—a minute longer and we had been too late—see how the east already glitters with streaks of gold—see how the twilight vanishes over the hills and woods—see what thousands of dew-drops sparkle with the rays of morning, and listen to the notes of birds innumerable, warbling their early songs! Oh, Alonzo! My God is great!—My breast is too contracted for all my feelings!—Burst forth,—burst forth, ye tears of transport which stand in my eyes!—Rejoice with me, my love; behold where the God ascends in unclouded majesty—he is not offended. (*She kneels.*) Father, to whose service I have devoted myself!—Father, whose image I bear externally on my bosom, and internally in my heart!—Vouchsafe to cast one of thy many eyes upon me, be witness of my love for this young man, and be my judge!—If the feelings which now engross my soul be sinful, then veil thy flaming forehead in darkness, or command thy thunder-clouds to gather round thee, and send down upon me thy forked lightning, as the minister of thy vengeance!—Give me, oh Father!—Give me a sign of thy love or of thy anger!—(*After a pause*) Oh with what mildness, what gentleness, do his rays fall upon me!—how benignantly he looks down and blesses me!—(*She rises*) Well then I dare venture upon the trial—dare venture to make it even in the presence of my God himself!—Alonzo, come to my arms. (*She embraces him*) It is over, and now all my fears are dispelled!—Had this embrace been sinful, he had annihilated us both at this moment!—My heart is full of joy and gratitude!— Come let us kneel together!—together pray—together give thanks!

Alonzo. I pray with thee?—Dear Cora, the sun is not my God.

Cora. Oh yes, he is equally yours and mine. Does he not shine upon all?—to all give light and warmth?—I entreat you, kneel with me.

Alonzo. Dear Cora!

Cora. Ungrateful man!—to whom do you owe your Cora?—Would I in the presence of my God be ashamed of you, my Alonzo?—Oh then if indeed you love me!—(*She kneels and takes his hand to draw him after her.*)

Alonzo. Who could resist such sweet enthusiasm! (*He kneels by her.*)

Cora. Let silent thanks,—the inward emotions of our hearts be the only incense we offer.

Alonzo. These I present to thee, God of all gods! (*They both remain in silent prayer.*)

SCENE III.—*Enter* ROLLA *from his Cave.*

Is it so early!—The sun is scarcely risen!—Alas, thus he sets and rises again, yet ever finds me wakeful!—But let me arm myself with patience, and the time will shortly come when he will find me sleeping for ever!—(*He sees Don Juan and Diego*) Who have we here?—two of the strangers who live among us—doubtless they have lost their way among these bushes, and have been overtaken by the night. I will awake them, and present them with refreshments;—yet first let me offer my morning prayers to thee, my Father!

ROLLA *turns to the East, and as he raises his hands and eyes towards Heaven, suddenly espies the lovers kneeling upon the hill, at sight of whom, he utters a shriek of horror, and remains immoveable as if he had seen a spirit.* CORA *and* ALONZO *rise slowly with their faces still turned towards the sun, and sink into a silent embrace.* ROLLA *overpowered, exclaims with a voice almost suffocated with anguish,* "CORA!!!" *The lovers start affrighted, turn round, and look down*——CORA *sinks in a swoon upon the declivity of the hill.*———ALONZO *after hesitating a few moments whether to hasten down, or stay and assist* CORA, *at length decides on the latter, kneels by her, and endeavours to recover her.* ROLLA *trembling with agony, yet unable to stir from the spot, remains with his eyes fixed upon the lovers.* ALONZO *at length exclaims* Velasquez! Diego! to arms! to arms! (JUAN *and* DIEGO *spring up, but are scarcely awake.*)

Juan. What is the matter?

Diego. What is the matter?

Alonzo. Seize him!—Don't let him escape!

Juan and Diego. (*Still staggering with sleep, yet endeavouring to draw their swords*) Where! whom!

Alonzo. Seize him! secure him! he will escape!

Juan. (*Recovering himself, and pointing to Rolla*) That man? that single man?

Diego. (*Brandishing his sword*) Two to one!—I am your man for that!

Alonzo. Secure him I say! we are betrayed!

Juan. A single unarmed man! (*He returns his sword into the scabbard.*)

Alonzo. (*Quitting Cora, who is not yet recovered, draws his sword and rushes down the hill towards Rolla, who keeps his eyes immoveably fixed upon Cora*) Then I must myself.—

Juan. (*Seizing him by the arm*) Hold, my friend—or rather my enemy, if you move a step.

Alonzo. My God, Velasquez, have you lost your senses? We are betrayed! you risk Cora's life! (*Endeavouring to break away from him.*)

Juan. (*Eagerly thrusting him back*) Restrain your passion! (*He goes up to Rolla.*) Surely you are not unknown to me.—Is it not Rolla whom I behold?

Rolla. (*Somewhat recovering himself.*) I—who am I? Yes, my name is Rolla.

Juan. Rolla, the champion of his country?—Yes, it is he, and in him I salute one of the bravest and noblest of men.

Rolla. How is this? it is yet early morning! (*Striking his hand upon his forehead.*) Am I in a dream? (*After a pause, and fixing his eyes again stedfastly upon Cora*) No!—By all the gods it is no dream?

Juan. Oh no!—Howsoever severe may be the censure which your eyes denounce against the scene before you—in how horrible a light soever you may be inclined to consider the truth, still it must be owned that this is no dream. Probably you may recognize that maiden by the figure of your deity which adorns her bosom. She is a VIRGIN OF THE SUN.

Rolla. And her name is Cora.

Juan. This young man too, you may also recollect—he is the favourite of your king, that Alonzo who saved the life of Ataliba at Cannara, while Rolla was fighting in support of his throne under the walls of Cuzco.

Rolla. (*Offering his hand to Alonzo*) Yes, it is the same Alonzo.

Juan. And now, Rolla, if you be indeed the man I believe you, your sentiments and feelings must differ widely from those of your priests, who having their eyes almost continually fixed upon the sun, when they chance to look downward towards the earth, see all things here below through a false medium, so that scarcely any object appears under its proper form and colour. You know the world, and mankind, know how the heart is eternally swayed by circumstances, now this way, now that, and what numberless passions contend for sovereignty within it. Among these, Love is always resisted with the greatest difficulty—indeed is scarcely to be withstood, but where, in making the attack, he has not deigned to exert all his powers. Look at that virgin—she is lovely——

Rolla. Great God!—to whom is this observation addressed.

Juan. Look at this youth—he is ardent, impetuous. That he saw and loved her is his only crime.

Rolla. It is no crime.

Juan. There spake Rolla!—I was not deceived in him!—

Alonzo. And you will keep our secret?—will avert, nameless, misery from the unfortunate Cora?

Rolla. Think you, that I could betray her?—Know, young man, that for years I have loved, have idolized her.

Alonzo and Juan. (*At the same moment and with the utmost astonishment*) You!!!

Rolla. Oh the impotence of words!—Not my language—not your language—not all the languages of the world combined, have power to describe what I feel for Cora?—She was scarcely above the age of childhood when I marched for the first time against the rebels who inhabit the fields at the foot of the mountains of Sangay—she wept when I bade her adieu, and since our separation, I have known no pleasure but in the recollection of that moment and of those tears. When the contest was ended, I returned, but all had then assumed a new aspect. No longer was I to behold the same free unfettered maiden whom I had left, she was become the confident of the gods. I would have made her my wife, she saw the purity of the flame with which I burned, she saw the ardour of my passion, but her heart was wholly occupied with her new situation, and while she called the sun her husband, she looked down with contempt upon me. The day soon arrived on which a solemn oath consecrated her for ever to the service of her God, and consigned me over as a victim to eternal misery. Still I continued for several years to drag about a miserable existence from place to place, from battle to battle, and while I sought death gained only renown. At length I retired to this spot, and for some weeks past, this cave has been my dwelling.—This cave, which has become dear to me since it conceals from my sight that sun who robbed me of my Cora!

Alonzo. (*Who during this narrative has again hastened to Cora, and endeavoured, though still in vain, to recover her.*) I pity you from my soul!—believe me I pity you from my soul!—But how can I trust a rival?—Swear that you will not betray us.

Rolla. I will not swear.

Alonzo. No!—and yet you pretend to love Cora?

Rolla. What need of oaths since I do love her?

Alonzo. For the satisfaction of my mind.

Rolla. What does your satisfaction concern me?

Alonzo. I entreat this of you!—Do you wish to keep me in incessant torments?—Would you force me to proceed to extremities?—recollect that cases may occur when the commission of an apparent crime, is in reality to perform an act of virtue.

Rolla. (*Contemptuously.*) Indeed!

Alonzo. And should I ever perceive the slightest ground for suspicion that thou wert capable of betraying Cora—observe, Rolla, though I respect and honour thee, yet I assure thee both by my God, and thy own, that I would take thy life without remorse.

Rolla. I will not swear.

Alonzo. Rolla, I entreat it once more!—What am I to think of this refusal?—See how I am shaken to my very soul—every limb trembles—my veins swell—and I can scarcely breathe for anguish. In mercy then swear.

Rolla. I will not swear.

Alonzo. (*Drawing his sword in a rage, and pressing upon Rolla.*) Die then!

Juan. (*Catching him hastily by the arm*) Is reason again gone astray?—Hold! hold!—are you a knight?

Alonzo. Stand off, or my sword shall dispatch thee also! (*He struggles to break away from Don Juan, while Rolla continues immoveable and unconcerned.*)

Juan. This storm of passion is too mighty for me!—I can restrain him no longer—Rolla, defend thyself!

Rolla. Seek not to restrain him, I die willingly for Cora! (*During this scene Cora recovers from her swoon, and as she opens her eyes perceives the struggle. She starts up with the wildest anguish, rushes hastily down the hill, and throws herself into Rolla's arms.*)

Cora. Alonzo, what would you do?

Alonzo. It is for thee!—for thy sake alone!—Should he betray thee, we are lost.

Cora. He betray me!—Rolla, my truest friend betray me!—He who was ever my defender, my intercessor, while I was yet a child,—who has so many times softened my mother's rage when I had offended her!—Oh Rolla, you must remember it well?

Rolla. But too well!

Cora. And do you think that he would betray me?

Alonzo. Why then did he refuse the oath I required?

Cora. Had you cause sufficient to require an oath?—Look at those eyes!—are they not a stronger security for his faith than any oath?

Rolla. (*Clasping her to his bosom.*) Now let me die!—Let me, oh ye gods, die this very moment!—I am so happy;—so blessed!—Cora reposes confidence in me, I clasp her in my arms, I hear her voice once more!—Ah, five years have elapsed since I experienced such happiness, since I saw her except at an awful distance.

Cora. (*Earnestly.*) And I rejoice no less to see you again so near me!—In your presence all the happy days of my childhood seem to pass anew before my eyes—so many delightful images are present to my recollection.——

Alonzo. (*Leaning upon his sword, and betraying emotions of the most poignant jealousy*) Cora, what torments do you inflict upon me!

Cora. Why are you tormented?—Oh you do not know how strong an affection I bear for Rolla!—When a youth he loved me, and we were destined for each other.—Yes, Rolla, is it not true that we were destined for each other?

Rolla. Oh true, true indeed!—for your virtuous mother—but no more—had she not died so prematurely—who knows—

Cora. Ah, dearest Alonzo, at that time I was continually turning his love into ridicule, because I knew not what it was to love. Forgive me, Rolla, I know it better now! Oh how often, and how grievously must I have tormented you!—

Rolla. Grievously!—most grievously!—but let that be forgotten—this moment is so truly blessed!—

Cora. Hear him, Alonzo, hear what kindness is breathed in every word he utters!—but my mother always told me the same—"*Rolla*," she repeatedly said, "*has one of the best of hearts—love him—marry him,—and I shall die happy.*"—But when she died, Rolla was engaged in fighting his sovereign's battles, and during his absence a sacred flame was kindled in my bosom.—At his return, therefore, I could not love him; my heart was devoted to my God, and I only sighed for the day when I should be wedded to the Sun.

Rolla. But this romantic enthusiasm has at length given way to nature, and love has found its way to your heart?

Cora. Yes, Rolla, that once insensible heart is insensible no longer—be you my confident.—I love that young man; our first meeting was in the Temple of the Sun, when I saw him standing by the side of our king.—My heart was instantly overpowered with an emotion for which I could scarcely account, and the dish that contained the bread of sacrifice, almost fell from my trembling hand. An ardent glance which he cast upon me, soon gave me assurance that my feelings were not unanswered on his part—yet since I was shut up within the boundaries of the Temple, and he could only steal round the outward walls, what hope remained that we might ever find the means of personally communicating our mutual passion. The gods saw and pitied our distress.—You must well remember that awful day, some months ago, when the hills around burst out with flames of fire,—when the ocean raged, and the earth trembled,—when many palaces were laid in ruins,—when even the Temple of the Sun itself was menaced with destruction, and the walls by which it is surrounded were rent asunder in two separate places. Then, trembling, and weeping, we poor affrighted servants of the gods ran hither and thither—death seemed to reign triumphant in our cells—he seemed still to pursue us when we fled under the roof of heaven alone, and our shrieks were mingled with the groans of contending nature. Alonzo, ever on the watch among these bushes, soon perceived the breach in the wall, and boldly ventured to ascend it—one stone after another fell beneath his feet—here the earth gaped to swallow him up, and there my arm was stretched out to receive him.—The darkness veiled our love from observation; and since that time my Alonzo has frequently found his way over the same ruins.

Rolla. Cora, I tremble for thee!—In what dreadful perils hast thou involved thyself!

Alonzo. Tell him all!—let him know the fatal consequence of *your* weakness, and *my* guilt!—tell him—

Cora. Yes, Rolla, it is true.

Rolla. What!—how!—Oh thoughtless girl!—And you, Alonzo, were you so ignorant of our customs that—ye gods!—ye gods!—my children you must fly!—instantly fly!

Juan. But whither?

Alonzo. Ah, Rolla, save her!

Cora. (*Terrified*) Is this really esteemed so high a crime here below, altho' the gods above do not regard it as an offence.

Rolla. How much my whole frame is shaken with horror!—I am at this moment scarcely capable of thought!—Cora, do you love him?

Cora. As my own soul.

Rolla. And are you certain that in his arms repentance will never corrode your peace, but that you can live and die contentedly as his wife?

Cora. 'Tis all I wish.

Rolla. And do you, Alonzo, feel the value of the sacrifice she would make you?

Alonzo. I feel it deeply.

Rolla. Then will I save you both. (*He places himself between them*) Come hither, and each give me a hand!—Consider me as your brother—as such, Cora, my dearest sister, I unite you to this man. (*Placing her hand in Alonzo's*) May the shade of your mother, which hovers over us at this moment, look down with an eye of favour upon your union!—May it be followed by her blessing—If you are happy, I shall be so. (*He turns aside, and wipes tears from his eyes.*)

Alonzo and Cora. (*Throwing their arms round him*) Our dearest brother!

Rolla. Yes, your brother!—and as your brother, will I pass the remainder of my days with you. In a sequestered spot, on the other side of the blue mountains, lives a friend of mine, an old Cazique, who, under the monarch of Cuzco, rules a mild and gentle race, many of whom served in their sovereign's army during the last war. At that time the son of the Cazique, a youth of the fairest promise, was severely wounded, and fell a prisoner into my hands; but, by my care and attention, he soon recovered of his wounds, and I restored him, without ransom, to his father. Since that moment the good man has been unbounded in his expressions of gratitude—He will receive us with transport; and in that remote province your love will find a secure asylum. There will I live with you,—tend and educate your children—be cheerful and happy, since Cora will be happy;—and at last, amid your brotherly and sisterly tears, quit this world with calmness and serenity, and ascend with transport to our Father above.

Cora. Where you will be received by my mother with inexpressible transports of gratitude!

Alonzo. Noble, generous man!—Scarcely dare I raise my eyes towards you!

Juan. (*Half aside, endeavouring to conceal a tear*) By all the saints above, if that man be not a Christian, I myself will turn Heathen!

Rolla. Let us now consult together what further is to be done!—Flight is resolved on; but the time and manner of its accomplishment remain to be considered.

Diego. (*Who, during this whole scene has been looking about in different places, to see that all was safe, now comes forward hastily.*) I hear a rustling noise behind the walls, and sounds which appear like the whispering of two female voices.

Rolla. Hasten, hasten into my cave! (*As they are going Idali and Amazili appear coming through the breach in the wall, and looking about with great eagerness and curiosity.*)

SCENE IV.—*Enter* IDALI *and* AMAZILI.

Alonzo. We are too late, they are here already!

Idali. Cora! we were looking for you.

Cora. I am coming.

Rolla. Tarry a moment!—They have seen and heard us,—for God's sake! do not let them escape thus; we must win them over to our interest.

Juan. That were a task for a minister of state!—If this be accomplished, I shall be persuaded that Rolla is capable of conquering whole provinces, without a stroke of the sword.

Rolla. Nothing more easy!—Flatter them, they are women.

Juan. Lovely maidens! will you not come near?

Idali. (*To Amazili*) I believe he means to address us.

Amazili. How he fixes his eyes upon us!—Let us hasten back.

Idali. Come, Cora, the High-Priestess sent us to seek for you.

Alonzo. Pray come nearer, pious virgins!

Juan. And receive the homage due to your charms.

Idali. (*To Amazili.*) Shall we run away?

Amazili. Yes; let us fly. (*Neither of them stir.*)

Cora. I will go with you directly. But why do you stand there so bashfully among the trees?—Come here, sisters.

Idali. Oh no, not among men.

Juan. Men!—Fair maidens! how came you to suppose us men? Three of us are only Spaniards, and the other will readily withdraw, if you wish to avoid his presence. (*He makes a sign to Rolla, who immediately retires into the entrance of his cave.*) Are you still afraid, sweet maidens?

Amazili. (*To Idali*) What do you think,—shall we venture?

Idali. You step first, and I will follow.

Amazili. No, you are the oldest.

Idali. But you got over the wall first.

Amazili. Yes; but it was you that first spied the breach.

Juan. The contest may easily be decided. (*He steps between them, and draws them both after him*) Now you may safely swear that neither took the first step.

Amazili. Ah, Idali! he has laid such fast hold of me!

Idali. And of me too!

Juan. Be quiet, dear children! no harm shall happen to you. (*He chucks Idali under the chin*) You are blooming as a rose. (*Turning to Amazili*) And you, as—as—as—

Diego. (*With great gallantry*) As a sun-flower.

Juan. (*To Idali*) Your eyes are so soft and blue.

Diego. (*To Amazili*) Yours are so very roguish.

Juan. You smile so sweetly.

Diego. The coral of your lips is so alluring.

Juan. This hand is so soft.

Diego. This waist is so slender.

Amazili. (*To Idali*) Shall we run away?

Idali. I think we may as well stay a little.

Amazili. But are you certain that you are not men?—We must die if you deceive us.

Cora. Come, sisters, we shall be missed.

Idali. And then the High-Priestess will scold.

Amazili. We ought to be dressing for the festival.

Idali. And there is nobody in the temple—the sacred flame will be extinguished.

Diego. You can easily kindle it again with your bright eyes.

Cora. Tell me, Idali, how happened it that the High-Priestess sent you hither?

Idali. We repaired to the temple this morning to take your place, and not finding you there, we went and reported it to the High-Priestess, who immediately sent us to look for you in the garden.

Cora. Did she give you no further orders?

Amazili. Only when we found you, to send you to her.

Juan. And should she ask where you met with Cora, what will you answer?

Idali. That we found her talking with some Spaniards.

Juan. Oh you must not mention us, sweet girls! for the High-Priestess will be angry at your staying so long, and forbid your meeting us again—and you would like, I hope, to come here sometimes, and amuse us with your conversation.

Diego. (*To Amazili*) I have fallen so desperately in love with you, my little rogue, that I hope you will come and meet me again.

Amazili. (*To Idali*) What do you say, Idali?

Idali. I can't tell.

Juan. Say rather that Cora had fallen asleep behind one of the pillars in the temple, and in the dusk of morning you did not perceive her.

Diego. Or that she was lying under the shade of the great palm-tree, in the court before the temple.

Amazili. Oh charming!

Idali. An excellent thought!

Cora. Come, let us hasten back.

Idali. It is indeed time; let us go.

Amazili. Yes, let us go. (*Neither she nor Idali stir*)

Juan. Go sweet maiden.

Diego. Go you little rogue.

Idali. Well, good morning—good morning.

Amazili. Farewel—farewel. (*They return over the wall*)

Cora. (*Embracing Alonzo*) Farewel, Alonzo!

Alonzo. Farewel, my beloved—soon my wife. [*Exit Cora.*

SCENE V.—*Re-enter* ROLLA.

Rolla. Well, how have you managed them?

Diego. Most completely—we have wound them round our fingers.

Juan. Rolla knows their sex.

Rolla. By report chiefly.

Diego. I begin to like the adventure extremely—my little creature seemed disposed to be very loving.

Juan. Yet the clouds, so pregnant with thunder, every moment gather thicker over our heads, and wear a more menacing aspect.

Alonzo. (*Taking Rolla's hand*) Brother!—dearest brother hasten to extricate us!

Rolla. I must consider the matter more calmly.—Oh what new vigour have my limbs acquired!—I am become quite another man. No longer are all things indifferent to me; I find something again to interest me in the world; I can again hope and fear, desire and reject.—Thanks to thee, Cora, for the mild rain which has thus revived the withered plant. Yes, we will fly!—Flight may be dangerous, but I shall find it therefore the more grateful. When our pursuers shall be so close upon us, that their cries assail our ears, and their arrows fly around us, then shall I be inspired with new life. When Rolla shall fight for Cora—when he shall brandish his sword in her defence, then will be, indeed, the moment for displaying the full extent of his powers. I was called valiant under the walls of Cuzco, and in the fields of Tumibamba; but then I did not fight for Cora—did not fight under her eyes!—In that situation I shall become a god!

Alonzo. (*Falling on his neck*) Exalted man!—Deign to give me but one friendly glance as an assurance that you have pardoned the headstrong boy!

Rolla. No, Alonzo, I would not have more merit ascribed to me than I can justly claim. All that I do is for Cora—nothing for you. Were she only to drop a withered flower into the water, and express a wish to have it again, I would instantly plunge into the stream to recover it for her, even at the hazard of my life. It is for her sake alone that I am your friend—for *her* sake that I pardon *you.*

Alonzo. Yet permit me at least to cherish a hope, that I may one day be thought worthy of a place in your friendship, for my own sake.

Rolla. You are beloved by Cora, what more can you wish. Oh! if Cora loved *me,* the gods themselves might seek my friendship in vain!—But we are merely talking, when we ought to be in action. Come into my cave, there we shall be secure from listeners; there we can arrange the plan of our escape, and carouse together unmolested;—for to-day I am resolved to carouse— yes, even to intoxication!—I am already intoxicated—intoxicated with joy! From the crown of my head to the sole of my foot, every atom of my frame is in a commotion of extacy. My strength, my faculties, have acquired such additional power, that at this moment I seem as if I could controul the world! (*He takes Alonzo's hand, and leads him into his cave.*)

Juan. (*Following them*) Happy is it for the king of Quito that this man is in love. Either to love with such unbounded passion, or to precipitate his sovereign from his throne, seems to be the destination of such a mind. [*Exit.*

Diego. Drink, and carouse!—I am your man for that.—It shall quickly be seen who can empty his glass, to the honour of his girl, most frequently, and with the greatest expedition. [*Exit.*

END OF THE SECOND ACT.

ACT III.

SCENE I.—*The* HIGH-PRIESTESS'S *Apartment in a Building called the House of the Stars. Several Cages with Parrots, Turtle-Doves, and other Birds, are hanging or standing about the Room. The* HIGH-PRIESTESS *is employed in feeding the Birds.*

HIGH-PRIESTESS.

There, there, little Bibi!—You rogue you would devour every thing!—These girls are gone a long time, I suppose they are somewhere prattling together, upon some trifling subject, till they forget how time goes.—Wait a few minutes, Lulu,—your turn will come in time.—These tedious creatures put me out of all patience, Heaven knows what they are doing, they are as stupid as oysters, and as slow as tortoises.—Come hither, Dudu,—there take this, and give a bit to your wife—oh you little ingrate! you can bite, can you.—This is too much!—the sun is already risen above the hills, and they are not returned!—the giddy creatures rely too much upon the mildness and gentleness of my heart, don't they Bibi?—I am too ready to overlook a fault, am I not Lulu?—But locking them up for a while without food will tame them, and make them more tractable, won't it Dudu?

SCENE II.—*Enter* IDALI *and* AMAZILI *in haste and almost breathless. They both speak together.*

Idali and Amazili. Here we are already.

High-Priestess. Softly, softly, children!—Poor Bibi, are you frightened?—And so you are absolutely here already?

Idali. Oh yes, we have run all the way.

High-Priestess. Whence, then, do you come?

> *Idali.* From the garden. }
> > (*Both speaking together.*)
> *Amazili.* From the temple. }

High-Priestess. One of you must be guilty of a falsehood.

> *Idali.* It is I! }
> > (*Extremely terrified and speaking together.*)
> *Amazili.* It is I! }

High-Priestess. Why how now?—One of you have uttered an untruth again. What is at the bottom of all this?—Idali, do you remain where you are, and you, Amazili, come with me. (*She leads her to the other side of the Stage, and speaks in a half whisper*) Tell me truly, do you come from the temple?

Amazili. Yes.

High-Priestess. Now don't stir. (*She goes to Idali.*) Amazili positively asserts that you come from the garden, I can scarcely believe her—tell me the real truth.

Idali. Oh yes, we come from the garden.

High-Priestess. So, so!—Some pretty trick has been playing here, and I must sift out the truth as well as I can. Idali, don't stir from your corner.—And what is the meaning of all this winking, and nodding, and shaking of the head?—Keep your head still, and your eyes upon the ground. (*She goes to Amazili*) Have you found Cora?

Amazili. Yes.

High-Priestess. Where did you find her?

Amazili. She had fallen asleep under the large palm-tree that stands before the porch of the temple.

High-Priestess. Remain there, and don't take your eyes from the ground. (*She goes to Idali*) Have you found Cora?

Idali. Yes.

High-Priestess. Where did you find her?

Idali. Sitting behind a pillar in the temple, fast asleep. We might have passed her twenty times without perceiving her.

High-Priestess. Admirable!—Now both of you come hither. (*She takes a hand of each, and looks steadfastly first at one, then at the other*) You have both uttered falsehoods! You say that Cora was asleep behind a pillar in the temple, and you that she was under the palm-tree in the court of the temple. (*Idali and Amazili hem, and cough, and look terrified and embarrassed*) Which am I to believe?

Idali. (*To Amazili*) Silly girl, you have forgotten every thing.

Amazili. No, it is you who have forgotten.

Idali. No, indeed it is you.

Amazili. I am sure that I was bid to say under the shade of the great palm-tree.

Idali. I am sure I was bid to say behind the pillar.

High-Priestess. *I was bid!* and, *I was bid!*—What may all this mean? (*Idali and Amazili hesitate*) If you will not please to recollect yourselves now, I shall soon find a way to assist your memories.

Idali. (*To Amazili.*) This is your fault.

Amazili. No, it is your's.

Idali. I certainly did not mention him first.

High-Priestess. HIM!—who?—who?——Oh you wicked girls, why you have not been among men I hope?—The gods defend us from so horrible a misfortune!

Idali and Amazili. Oh no!—no indeed!

High-Priestess. No?

Idali. They were not men.

Amazili. Only Spaniards.

High-Priestess. Spaniards!—how?—what?—Spaniards!—(*She pauses and somewhat recovers herself.*) Well, well, if they really were only Spaniards?—And how many might there be?

Amazili. (*Growing pleased and communicative*) Three. One for Cora, one for Idali, and one for me. Mine, had fine brown hair, and eyes just the same colour.

Idali. Mine had black curling hair, and such a sweet countenance.

Amazili. But mine was the handsomest.

Idali. No, mine was much handsomer.

High-Priestess. Well, well, this may be settled another time. Now tell me how came these Spaniards in the temple?

Idali. They were not in the temple.

High-Priestess. What, then; had they flown over the high walls into the garden?

Idali. They were not in the garden.

Amazili. But they might have come in, as easily as we got out.

High-Priestess. You got out of the garden?—and how could that be managed?

Idali. According to your orders we went to look for Cora. We ran hither and thither, and called her by her name, but to no purpose, till at last as we were looking about, and listening, we thought we heard voices on the other side of the wall, just by the arbour, where the little stream is lost in the wood. We followed the sound, and crept softly through the thick bushes, till at last we came to a great, great rent in the wall, from the top, quite to the bottom, and so broad that Amazili and I could easily go through it, and we had only to step over a few stones to get quite on the outside.

High-Priestess. And you did step over the stones and get on the outside?

Amazili. Else we should not have found Cora.

High-Priestess. Indeed!—What, she too had stepped over the stones?

Idali. Yes, and was talking with the Spaniards. At first we thought they were men, and were going to run away, but they entreated us very earnestly to stay; and as we found that they really were only Spaniards, we thought there could be no harm in complying with them.

Amazili. And they wanted us to promise that we would come again.

High-Priestess. Which promise you made?

Idali. We only half promised it.

High-Priestess. But you intend meeting them again?

Amazili. What do you say, Idali?

Idali. Perhaps so, if you are inclined, Amazili.

High-Priestess. Well, well, at present go and send Cora hither—then dress yourselves, prepare the bread of sacrifice, and dispose it in the baskets.

Idali. (*Taking Amazili's hand*) Come, sister, I have such an inclination to dance.

Amazili. And I could laugh and sing. (*Exeunt both.*)

High-Priestess. (*Alone*) Dance, laugh, and sing, if you please, your simplicity protects you from my anger;—but you shall not find the breach in the wall again, that I promise you. As for this, Cora—can the shameless creature have been carrying on an intercourse with men?—Chaste Oello, look down with compassion upon thy servants, and avert from us this last of all calamities!—I have long observed, that she has hung down her head—that her ruddy cheeks have lost their colour—that she has appeared abstracted, full of thought, and seemed scarcely to know with whom she was speaking, or to hear when she was addressed.—All this indicates no good, does it Dudu?

SCENE III.—*Enter* CORA.

High-Priestess. Shameless girl, do you dare to appear in my presence?

Cora. I come from the service of our god.

High-Priestess. Be thankful that his thunder is not entrusted to my hands.

Cora. What do you mean?—how have I incurred your anger?

High-Priestess. Do you suppose that I am unacquainted with your licentious conduct?—that I am ignorant how Cora disgraces these sacred walls, and exposes her own, and her sister's honour to censure.

Cora. I have done nothing wrong.

High-Priestess. Look stedfastly in my face,—you have been in the company of men?

Cora. I have not offended the gods.

High-Priestess. Cora, I command you to look at me!—you are acquainted with a Spaniard?

Cora. I am innocent.

High-Priestess. This very morning you have seen and conversed with him?

Cora. The sun was witness of all my actions.

High-Priestess. Confess your crime.

Cora. I have not been guilty of a crime.

High-Priestess. Oh blinded, misguided creature!

Cora. The path which I pursue, is that of nature and innocence.

High-Priestess. Obstinate girl!—But remember that you are a priestess of the sun, and tremble at the torments to which the severity of our laws destines those by whom they are transgressed.

Cora. I shall suffer undeservedly.

High-Priestess. You will not confide in me?

Cora. No.

High-Priestess. Nor confess your fault?

Cora. No.

High-Priestess. I admonish you for the last time, Cora!—But a few moments remain, in which confession is left to your choice—make your use of them. I know all—I am instructed in every particular. Soon shall I assemble the Virgins in the Temple, and convene thither the priests, who shall judge you, and by whom you will be judged with severity. Death will then be your lot, and worse than death, shame. At present we are alone,—do you persist in silence?

Cora. Yes.

High-Priestess. (*Changing her tone*) Enough, I cannot believe Cora to be really so guilty. I knew your mother, when you were yet a child, we had frequent intercourse with each other.—"*My Cora*," she would often say, "*has a gentle and complying spirit, for which quality I love her most tenderly.*"

Cora. Oh, she was always an affectionate mother!—All the happiness of my life was buried in her grave.

High-Priestess. You have doubtless a sacred reverence for her memory?

Cora. Can that be made a question!—Alas how many are the tears which I have shed for her in secret.

High-Priestess. If such your affection, you surely would not convict her of a falsehood, as she rests in her grave. Must I be compelled to think that it was only the blindness of maternal love which could ascribe to you this gentle and complying disposition?—or will you convince me that she was right in her judgment?

Cora. She was right!

High-Priestess. Then prove it to me. The mother's friend has an undoubted claim upon the daughter's confidence.

Cora. Ah me!—

High-Priestess. The last words that were uttered by her pallid lips, still vibrate in my ears. "*My child*" she said, "*is young and inexperienced, should she ever want maternal counsel, be it received from you!*"—She spoke,—with her cold hands pressed mine, and expired. (*Cora betrays symptoms of irresolution, and appears combating with herself. The High-Priestess continues after a pause*) And your aged and reverend father, when he gave you into my hands, kissed you and said, "*Take her, she is a good girl, and will not occasion you any trouble.*"—Afterwards, when he was about to return home, when he gave you his last blessing, while a tear trembled on his grey eye-lashes, what were his parting words—"*Cora, honour her as a mother.*"

Cora. (*Falling at her feet*) I love!

High-Priestess. (*Starting with horror*) You love?

Cora. I can no longer remain a priestess of the Sun!

High-Priestess. No longer remain a priestess of the Sun?

Cora. But will marry.

High-Priestess. Marry!—*you* marry!

Cora. The gods have given me a feeling heart.

High-Priestess. To be devoted to their service.

Cora. I was born to become a wife.

High-Priestess. The Sun is your husband.

Cora. To him I can offer only prayers and thanks; but our heart and our love can be bestowed only on a husband.

High-Priestess. Cora, recollect yourself, you are in a dream.

Cora. I have now laid open my whole soul. If the affection you bore the mother be indeed transferred to the daughter, you will be my friend.

High-Priestess. And the person you love is a Spaniard?

Cora. Yes.

High-Priestess. His name?—

Cora. Is Alonzo.

High-Priestess. When, and where, did you first see him?

Cora. In the Temple, by the side of our king.

High-Priestess. And what miracle brought you to a nearer intercourse?

Cora. The natural miracle which threatened the Temple with destruction, and rent asunder the walls by which it is enclosed.

High-Priestess. Well, I must not know more, and let what has passed be buried in eternal oblivion. To shew you in how high regard I hold your mother's memory, I will preserve your secret inviolate, and you must by severe repentance endeavour to avert the wrath of the gods. Erase the image of Alonzo from your heart, forget his smooth and deceitful tongue, think of him no more, but attend to your employments and devotions.

Cora. You certainly have never loved?

High-Priestess. No, thanks be to the gods!

Cora. Had you ever felt one half of what I now feel, you would have known that what you enjoin is no longer in my power. Erase the image of Alonzo from my heart!—think of him no more!—When I awake in the morning, he is always the first object of my thoughts, and at night when I lie down he is still the last.—When I kneel in the temple, his name intrudes itself into my prayers,—when I look at the image of the sun, I see only him,—and when I would turn my thoughts to my God, I cannot detach them from Alonzo.

High-Priestess. These are heavy offences, Cora!—You must fast, pray, humble yourself.

Cora. I can pray for nothing but that the gods may grant me Alonzo. Love is so soft, so exquisite a sensation that it never can be sinful.

High-Priestess. Sinful!—It is to be held in the utmost abhorrence.

Cora. Are *you* then so entirely free from all emotions of this passion.

High-Priestess. I am wholly devoted to the gods.

Cora. In this assertion you either deceive me or yourself. Do I not often see how tenderly you nurse and feed these birds,—taking, now this, now that, out of the cage, setting it on your finger, stroking it, kissing it, talking to it?

High-Priestess. Poor little creatures, to love them is such an innocent affection.

Cora. And my love is equally innocent.

High-Priestess. Love for a man!

Cora. The feeling is still the same!—the heart must love!—a turtle-dove engages your affections,—am I to blame if mine are fixed on other objects.

High-Priestess. Do not deceive yourself, Cora. Is it a matter of indifference, whether you employ the sacred flame only in consuming the sacrifice, or use it to set the temple on fire?

Cora. I do not comprehend your simile, my heart speaks in a plain and simple manner. I always thought that love must be pleasing to the gods, I have made the experiment, and the event has justified my opinion. The gods cannot be offended with me; for say, good mother, when Cora serves in the temple, does a sudden gloom overcast the heavens, does the sun conceal himself behind a cloud?

High-Priestess. No, your guilty course has been pursued only in darkness—the rays of the great light have never witnessed your crimes.

Cora. Yes, they also have witnessed my love. On this very morning I solemnly embraced Alonzo in the presence of the sun himself.

High-Priestess. (*With a start of horror*) Embraced Alonzo?

Cora. Pressed my lips, my breast, to his.

High-Priestess. Your lips—your breast!

Cora. And our god smiled upon us.

High-Priestess. No more, unhappy girl!—Go and conceal yourself before I repent that I made you a promise of secrecy. It is not *your* honour alone that is concerned in this affair, it is the honour of our whole order.—Go, and settle as well as you can with your heart, whether it may find the extinction of your passion pleasing, or displeasing; only of this be allured, that you must see Alonzo no more.

Cora. (*Resolutely*) I will no longer remain a priestess of the sun.

High-Priestess. Vain resolution!—Death only can release you from his service.

Cora. But you say that I am criminal.—Well, then, I am no longer worthy to serve the sun. If however I devote to him in my place, an innocent creature, pure and free from sin, will not this be pleasing to him, shall I not then have discharged my duty, and be released from my oath.

High-Priestess. I do not understand you.

Cora. The innocent creature which I bear within me shall be devoted to the sun. (*The High-Priestess starts back, attempts to speak, but is unable; she totters and is obliged to support herself against a chair*) What is the matter?—Have you misunderstood me?—The innocent creature which I bear within me shall be devoted to the sun.

High-Priestess. (*Running about in a phrenzy*) Idali!—Amazili!—Runa!—Ye daughters of the Sun, hasten hither!—Ah!—I cannot support myself!—(*She sinks down upon a chair*)

SCENE IV.—*Enter* IDALI, AMAZILI, *and several other* VIRGINS OF THE SUN *from different parts.*

All talking together. What is the matter?—What has happened?—She is in a swoon!—Cora, tell us what is the matter?—What has thrown her into this agitation?

Cora. (*With great composure*) I do not know.

High-Priestess. (*Recovering*) Hasten, ye daughters of the Sun, shut up this sacrilegious creature in our darkest dungeon, that the rays of our god may not be profaned by falling upon a being so contaminated. You Runa, and Odila must answer with your lives for the prisoner, till the moment when she shall be brought forth to judgment. The rest of you veil yourselves in the deepest mourning, and follow me to the royal palace. The Sun is incensed against us!—the wrath of the gods has lighted upon us!—heavy sins are to be answered!—curses must fall upon Peru, and the avenging arm of the powers above will pursue us into the most secret places. Hasten!—extinguish the sacred light in the temple, tear down the wreaths of flowers, no festival can now be solemnized, this day is changed into a day of mourning!—Let us repair to the foot of the throne to demand vengeance, dreadful vengeance against the criminal! (*She rushes out, a confused noise and murmuring is made by all present who all at once question Cora*)

All. What have you done, Cora?—Tell us?—Tell us?—

Cora. I have done nothing wrong. (*Exit with composure.*)

All. (*As they follow her*) Look well to her!—Take care that she does not escape!—Your lives must answer it! Away—away! (*Exeunt.*)

SCENE V.—*A large hall in the king's palace, with guards ranged on each side. Enter the* KING'S CHAMBERLAIN.

Chamberlain. (*To the Guards*) Throw open the doors!—Let all enter, who are come hither on this solemn day of festival to salute their sovereign the first-born of the sun, and conduct him to the temple. As soon as the king shall be arrayed in his Inca's robes, he will appear himself.

SCENE VI.—*The doors are thrown open. Enter the* HIGH-PRIEST, XAIRA, DON ALONZO, DON JUAN, *with a long train of priests and courtiers. Many compliments are exchanged on all sides; they walk about, and converse in different groupes. Several of the courtiers assemble round the chamberlain.*

Xaira. (*To the High-Priest.*) Why do these strangers come hither?

High-Priest. Probably to attend the king when he goes to the sacrifice.

Xaira. Oh impious, to permit the presence of strangers at the celebration of our solemnities, perhaps only to make them the subject of their mockery.

High-Priest. Mockery!—No, that were to shew themselves fools, and I can rely upon that brave youth for not being guilty of any folly. Have you forgotten that our king is indebted to him for his life—that he has made the people of Quito the terror of their enemies since he taught them the mode of fighting practised in his country—that he has also instructed us in many useful arts of peace?

Xaira. Mere deception. He has only increased our wants.—We were much happier without him.

High-Priest. Discontented man!

Chamberlain. Gentlemen, do you know any news for the entertainment of the king?

One of the Company. None, excepting that old Telasco arrived here yesterday evening from his province.

Another. And has brought his son Zorai to present him to the Inca.

Chamberlain. How long is it since the venerable old man last visited the capital?

First Speaker. Two years. He has not been here since he brought his daughter Cora to be consecrated as a Priestess.

Alonzo. (*Starting, and speaking aside to Juan*) Velasquez, do you hear that Cora's father is in Quito?

Juan. Yes, I hear it.

Alonzo. And her brother?

Juan. I hear that too.

Alonzo. This alone was wanting to make my misery complete!—How will their unsuspecting features harrow my conscience. (*Martial instruments are heard behind the scene, playing a march.*)

All. The king approaches.

SCENE VII.—*Enter* ATALIBA *with his train. All present prostrate themselves before the king.*

Ataliba. (*Addressing the High-Priest.*) I rejoice, good old man, to see how much your strength bears up beneath the weight of years.

High-Priest. Under such a sovereign one cannot grow old.

Ataliba. For what I am. I have solely to thank you; that I can never forget. (*To Xaira.*) It is a charming day, Xaira, the gods are favourably disposed towards us.

Xaira. (*With hesitation*) Yet—unfavourable omens, have disquieted my bosom.

Ataliba. How so?

Xaira. The lamb which I was about to sacrifice at midnight, struggled beneath the sacred knife.

Ataliba. Most natural.

Xaira. And the lungs, which, when they tremble and quiver after they are torn out, promise happiness for the ensuing year, lay still and motionless.

Ataliba. I thank you for the information, but I desire that it may not be spread abroad among the people. (*To the High-Priest, smiling and speaking in a half whisper.*) We have tygers enough to annoy us, why should we tremble before a lamb?

High-Priest. To the people such a lamb is more formidable than a tyger; and the king owes respect to popular faith.

Ataliba. True, good old man, for it was upon that foundation that Manco-Capac erected his dominion.—(*Turning to Alonzo.*) I rejoice, my beloved friend, to see that you are still contented to live among us.

Alonzo. How can I be otherwise, royal Inca, while you continue to entertain me thus hospitably?

Ataliba. Which I shall never cease to do, as long as I behold you so worthy of my love. (*To Velasquez*) Well, Don Juan, do the troops that you are training make a rapid progress?

Juan. They are brave fellows;—they have arms of iron, and hearts of wax.

Ataliba. Oh that I could be certain of enjoying eternal peace!—then should those nervous arms be devoted to agriculture alone. (*Turning to the High-Priest.*) Is it not time that we go to the Temple?

High-Priest. We are all ready.

Chamberlain. (*Approaching the king.*) Sire, the old Telasco, governor of the castle of Antis, is arrived, and wishes to pay his homage to the first-born of the Sun.

Ataliba. My worthy Telasco!—Let him come in.

Alonzo. (*Aside to Velasquez*) Oh Juan!—my heart! my heart!

Juan. Do not betray yourself.

SCENE VIII.—*On a signal from the Chamberlain, the Guards open the door, when* TELASCO, *and* ZORAI, *enter.*

Ataliba. (*Meeting and embracing Telasco.*) Welcome venerable old man!—What brings you from your enviable solitude into the bustle of a court? (*Calling to the Attendants.*) Let a seat be brought.

Telasco. Suffer me to stand, good Inca. It is the posture which best becomes a petitioner.

Ataliba. Has Telasco any request to make?—Speak then.

Telasco. Two years ago I brought my daughter here, to devote her, according to her own desire, to the service of the gods. I cannot deny that the parting with her was a severe trial to me, for I had long been accustomed to enjoy her innocent society, and ever since the death of my wife, when I fell into ill health, had been nursed and attended by her with the tenderest care and affection. It may be supposed, therefore, that we did not separate without many tears on both sides. My son, at that time a youth, was then the only treasure remaining—he is now grown up to manhood, and as his sister is devoted to the gods, I would devote him to the service of his country. To you, great king, I present him—be you his father when I am gone!—I do not doubt that he will conduct himself worthily—I have no fear he will ever forget that the blood of the Incas flows through his veins. Accept my present with favour!—I bring you the greatest treasure that I possess upon earth!—I bring you my all!

Ataliba. He shall be my own son!—Come hither, young man. (*Zorai kneels to him*) Inherit thy father's virtues, and thou shalt be heir to thy father's honours.

Zorai. Pardon my silence. Time only can decide whether or no I shall deserve such favour.

Ataliba. Rise!—Alonzo, I consign him to thy care. Let him be enrolled among my life-guards, and learn of thee to fight and conquer.

Alonzo. (*Embarrassed*) Oh king! I will endeavour to gain his confidence.

Telasco. (*To Alonzo*) Art thou the man in whom the people bless the saviour of their Inca? Permit these old arms to embrace thee! (*He embraces Alonzo*) Thy fame has reached to the remotest parts of this nation—thy name is repeated with transport by our children's children!—Happy is my son in being placed under such a leader.

Alonzo. (*Extremely embarrassed and affected*) He shall be my brother.

Telasco. (*To Ataliba*) To your goodness am I indebted that the last moments of my life are made thus happy. Accept my grateful thanks!

(*A solemn march is heard playing at a distance*)

Ataliba. Now, my children, let us repair to the temple!—Come, Telasco, go on my right hand, and should you find the walk fatiguing, let me be your support!—Ah, how often have you supported me!

Telasco. Blessings on you worthy, Inca!

(*As they are preparing to go, the music, which had continued gradually to advance nearer, suddenly stops*)

Ataliba. (*Starting*) What means this?

Chamberlain. (*Rushing in trembling, and almost breathless*) Sire, the High-Priestess of the Sun approaches, with a long train of priestesses all clad in mourning, and uttering dreadful lamentations. Their cries pierce the very soul; while the people gather round them trembling, and observing them with silent awe and terror. (*The whole assembly appear in the utmost confusion: the king alone preserves his composure*)

Ataliba. Conduct them hither.

Alonzo. (*Aside to Juan*) Oh God, Velasquez, what can this portend!

Juan. You tremble, and look pale;—for shame; rouse yourself; shew yourself a man!

SCENE IX.—*Enter the* HIGH-PRIESTESS, *followed by a long train of* VIRGINS OF THE SUN. *They are clad in thick mourning veils, and march in slow and solemn procession towards the King. An awful silence is observed by the whole company, who wait the sequel of the scene with anxious expectation.*

High-Priestess. (*Throwing back her veil*) Oh woe! woe! woe!

Ataliba. On whom dost thou imprecate woe?

High-Priestess. The temple is polluted!—the altars are profaned!—the holy lamp is extinguished!—Oh woe! woe! woe!

Ataliba. Name the criminal, that the gods may be avenged for these heavy offences.

High-Priestess. First born of the Sun, let the stringed instruments, let the festal song, cease!—Let the temple be divested of its ornaments, and the garlands be taken from the beasts prepared for sacrifice; to-day can no festival be solemnized!—Lamentations must be our only songs, mourning veils our only ornaments!—A serpent has with his poison polluted the house of the Stars!—A Virgin of the Sun has broken her vow of chastity! (*She pauses a few moments—the whole assembly shudder—Alonzo appears like one thunderstruck—at length the High-Priestess proceeds*) Woe! woe! upon CORA!!!

(*At the mention of this name the* KING *utters a cry of agony.*—TELASCO, *trembling, supports himself upon his staff*—ZORAI, *full of confusion, conceals his face in his garments*—ALONZO *is sinking to the ground, but is supported by Velasquez*—*A confused murmur is heard among the rest of the assembly.*)

High-Priestess. Vengeance! vengeance! upon the murderer of virtue!—upon the wretch who could abuse the hospitality of a peaceable people, and violate the sacred asylum of the Wives of the Sun!—Woe! woe! upon ALONZO!!!

(ATALIBA *utters a more piercing cry than before*—ALONZO *stands with downcast eyes, while a death-like paleness overspreads his countenance*—*The attention of the whole company is immediately turned towards him*—TELASCO *looks around with a vacant stare.*)

High-Priestess. First born of the Sun!—image of our God upon earth!—I stand here, and require from thee an awful atonement for this sacrilege!

Ataliba. (*With deep gloom*) Which thou shalt have.

High-Priestess. Be death and shame the lot of the seducer!—Be death and shame the lot of Cora, and her whole family!

(TELASCO *starts, murmurs to himself the word* "shame," *and falls to the ground—* ZORAI *throws himself by him.*)

Ataliba. All-merciful God! (*Calls to the attendants*) Come to the assistance of this poor old man. (*Telasco is raised up—the High-Priestess is about to proceed, but the King makes her a sign to be silent, and addresses her and her train*) Enough, ye pious women! I know my duty, and will perform whatever may be required by the ordinances of Manco-Capac. To question you, Alonzo, concerning the truth of the charge alledged against you, were needless;—thy death-like countenance, thy downcast eyes confess the fault too plainly, and thou art lost beyond the possibility of redemption.—Hadst thou excited my provinces to rebel against me; had thy sword deprived me of half my kingdom, I would have given thee my hand, and said, thou didst once save my life, and all that I have I share willingly with thee!—But now, the king alone must speak; the friend must remain silent.—Alonzo, thou art lost beyond the possibility of redemption!—Unhappy youth, what hast thou done!

Alonzo. Let me die!—Death is no more than I justly deserve, for having repaid with such base ingratitude the unmixed happiness I have enjoyed in this kingdom. Yes, let me die, oh king! (*Falling upon his knees*) But save, save, the hapless Cora!—she is innocent!—her seducer only is guilty!

Ataliba. Rise!—My power is confined within certain limits: and in no respect is it so rigidly circumscribed as in all matters which concern religion. (*He stands for some moments wrapt in mournful musing, and apparently struggling with himself, then says, with averted countenance*) Guards, put him in irons! (*To the High-Priest*) Assemble your priests in the court of the temple, to judge the culprits according to our holy laws and customs; and ere the sun sink into the ocean, let me be summoned to confirm the sentence. (*Going*)

Xaira. Sire, it is necessary the father and brother should also be put in irons.

Ataliba. Poor old man!—he will not run away from you!

Xaira. The brother at least.

Ataliba. Well, if it must be!—(*Zorai is put in irons*) Oh what misery is it to be king when one is compelled to punish! (*Exit*)

High-Priestess. (*To the High-Priest*) Hasten, thou first servant of our gods, hasten to avenge your masters, that this very evening the last rays of the declining sun may beam upon the grave which encloses Cora—Go, ye daughters of the sun, bow yourselves down in prayer, wash the altar with your tears, and conceal your blushing cheeks beneath sevenfold veils, till the disgrace with which our Order has been branded by that profligate stranger, be wholly effaced!—(*Exit, followed by the Virgins of the Sun*)

High-Priest. (*Aside*) Poor Rolla! (*Exit*)

Xaira. (*To some of the other Priests*) Go out at the northern gate, and prepare a grave in that waste and desolate spot which is distinguished by numerous heaps of stones.

Telasco. And let me be the first laid within it! [*Exeunt Priests.*

Xaira. (*To the Guards*) Lead the prisoners away.

Alonzo. (*To Juan*) Farewel, Velasquez!—When you return to our native country, bear my tenderest greetings to my poor mother; but be careful to conceal from her my unhappy story.

Telasco. (*As he is seized by the guards*) Whither would you drag me, old as I am?

Alonzo. Oh, Velasquez, this old man!—this unfortunate old man!

Telasco. Give me my daughter!—restore me my daughter!

Xaira. Away with them all.

Telasco. (*As he is led off*) Give me my daughter!—restore me my daughter! [*Exeunt omnes.*

END OF THE THIRD ACT.

ACT IV.

SCENE I.—*A barren Spot on the Outside of the Walls of the Temple. Four* PRIESTS *are employed in making a Grave;—several other* PRIESTS *are scattered about. While they sing the first Chorus,* ROLLA *appears upon the Stage.*

(*Solemn Chorus of Priests.*)

Haste!—dig with eager hands a grave,

Our guiltless heads from death to save!

A grave, to turn from us aside

The darts destruction's daemons guide!

For hark!—both justice and compassion cry,

"To save the guiltless, let the guilty die!"

Rolla. (*Starting*) What do I hear!—say,—what is the meaning of this?

(*Chorus of Priests.*)

Haste!—dig a grave t'avenge the gods!

A grave, that in death's dark abodes,

Lost Cora's crime, of deepest die,

May soon for ever buried lie!

Rolla. Cora's crime!—speak!—answer me!

A Priest. Away from this spot!—It is cursed for Cora's sake.

Rolla. Curses upon thyself, thou damned babbler!—But say!—why these solemn preparations?—for what miserable victim is this grave designed?

(*Chorus of Priests.*)

Brethren!—the grave's prepar'd!—away!

Bring Cora hither!—hence!—obey!—

That perishing in earth's dark womb

Which must her living form entomb,

She a sin-offering may become, for sin;

And by her sufferings heaven's compassion win.

Rolla. Ye powers above!—what sounds are these!—they fall like a mountain upon my head! (*The priests collect their tools, and prepare to depart*) Speak, ye flinty-hearted men!—speak!—speak!—it is Rolla who entreats you!—Rolla entreats!—One who is not accustomed to solicitation entreats you to tell him the meaning of what he sees!—What has happened here?—for what purpose is this grave prepared?—and why do you sing that ill-omened song? (*The priests are going, Rolla stamps on the ground*) Stop, and speak, or dread the violence you will provoke! (*Exeunt the Priests, Rolla is following them*)

The translator acknowledges her obligation to a friend, for the verification of these chorusses.

SCENE II.—DIEGO *enters in great haste, and extreme agitation.* ROLLA *stops on seeing him.*

Rolla. Ha!—Surely I recollect you, my friend!—Were not you also present at my late interview with Alonzo?—Tell me then what has happened since he departed hence?—speak!—instantly speak?

Diego. See, I tremble in every limb. My poor unfortunate master!—Ah, he languishes in chains!

Rolla. And Cora?—Cora?

Diego. Probably shares his fate.—Don Juan must know more, for he was present during the whole scene.

Rolla. Don Juan!—I thank you for mentioning his name!—Where is he?—hasten, hasten to seek him!—Conduct him hither instantly!—I will wait here to receive him.—Begone, I entreat you!—the moments are precious! (*Exit Diego*) My agony is intolerable!—I am impatient to know all, yet tremble at the thoughts of what I may hear!—I can scarcely breathe for anguish!—Uncle, uncle, where are you? (*Going*)

SCENE III.—*Enter the* HIGH-PRIEST.

Rolla. Ha!—here he is!—Oh tell me instantly, whether this be true or false?

High-Priest. Your words are scarcely intelligible, yet the wildness of your looks explains them but too clearly.—Alas! it is true!

Rolla. (*Pointing to the grave*) And here?

High-Priest. (*With a deep sigh, and turning away his face*) Yes!

Rolla. Tremble then, oh earth, and let thy whole surface become desolate!—Groan! groan! ye hills!—Thou fire burst forth in the valleys and consume the fruits of the soil, that the fertile spots may no longer be crowned with verdure, but the whole earth appear as one vast scene of conflagration!—Rise ye terrors of nature, ye storms and whirlwinds, that I may breathe more freely amid your mighty conflicts,—that the voice of my agony may contend with your roarings!—that my arm may slay more rapidly than the lightning itself!

High-Priest. Rolla, for the sake of all the gods!—

Rolla. No, she shall not die!—sooner shall the sacred lamp be extinguished, and the temple itself become a desert!—Believe me, Uncle, she shall not die!—you may tell me that the grave is already prepared—that her fate is inevitable!—Yes, it is prepared, but Rolla still lives!

High-Priest. Your words are of dreadful import!

Rolla. Sooner shall it be Rolla's grave!—sooner shall he be stretched upon the earth, senseless, motionless, a breathless corpse!—Yet let him not even then be trusted hastily!—examine carefully that every spark of life be really extinguished, since if only one be left smothering, it will assuredly burst forth into a flame, and consume the persecutors of Cora. Oh, while this hand can wield a sword, let no one venture to touch Cora!—the blood of him who should harbour so sacrilegious a thought, shall answer for his rashness!—the priests—the king—even thou thyself.

High-Priest. Madman rage on!—dare in thy phrenzy to raise thy arm against the gods!—

Rolla. Against the gods!—No, the gods are on my side, their lightning is in my hand, their shield before my breast!—Short-sighted mortals!—What are the brightest, warmest rays of our god but pure effusions of that benign love which alike unfolds the rose-bud, and expands the human heart. Woe then to the miserable wretch who remains insensible to its genial influence, and pining in a cold damp corner of the earth lives a life scarcely superior to the senseless oyster. Cora even excels her former self, since she has yielded to this impulse;—and how could she fail to do so, for the gods would never leave their master-piece unfinished; and what is the heart without love, but a lamp without light, an eye without the power of vision?——These are things, Uncle, which however *you* cannot understand.

High-Priest. You do me injustice, Rolla.

Rolla. Injustice!—You cannot have been yourself susceptible of the exquisite, the heavenly, feeling of love, when it is your lips that have condemned Cora.

High-Priest. You are right now—it was my *lips* condemned her.

Rolla. But not your heart?

High-Priest. Not my heart.

Rolla. Come then to my arms;—I rejoice to find that you are a man!—But why stand here so cold and inactive?—fly and save her!

High-Priest. That is impossible.

Rolla. Courage, dear Uncle, courage!—Your grey hairs, your mild eloquence, my sword, and the arm of God!—all these united—Yes, yes, we will save her!

High-Priest. Alas, young man, zeal blinds you to the steep rocks which lie in our way.

Rolla. I feel sufficient energy to defy them.

High-Priest. Ancient popular opinions—the customs of whole centuries——

Rolla. Nature is older than these.

High-Priest. But not more powerful.

Rolla. Mere evasion.

High-Priest. Could I, by sacrificing the few short years remaining of my life, redeem the hapless Cora's, I would instantly with firm and resolute step descend into this vault.

Rolla. Babble.

High-Priest. Are these tears also babble?

Rolla. Hypocrisy!—do not talk, but act.

High-Priest. What can I do?

Rolla. (*Raising his hands towards Heaven*) Oh Father above, do thou then interpose to save her!—suffer not the most perfect work upon which thy rays ever shone to be destroyed, but, to the confusion of these unfeeling priests, save her!—Oh, how could I expect to find a heart of sensibility within such a shell!—the heart that beats beneath those garments never can have any feeling, except for vain and senseless customs; it dissembles towards its god, and is blood-thirsty as a tyger's.

High-Priest. Oh Rolla, you know not how much you wrong me!

Rolla. Carefully instructed by your fathers and mothers to pluck every flower which might lie in your way,—to wring the neck of every bird which might fall into your hands,—from your infancy each avenue in your hearts has been closed against humanity, while he, who could with the greatest composure perform such ignoble actions, was considered as bearing in his bosom the germs of the future High-Priest.

High-Priest. This from you, Rolla?

Rolla. Beloved and pampered self is the sole object of your attention,—beauty is to you as a blunted arrow—and love appears an absurd romance. A shake of the head is the utmost tribute you can pay to the sufferings of a brother, nor does the tear of sympathy ever *start* into your eyes, it only quivers there by compulsion. No emotion of concern would intrude into your breast were the world itself to be laid in ruins, provided *you* were spared and could continue to live in case and affluence.

High-Priest. Rolla, you torture me—you break my heart!—I must speak out and shame you.

Rolla. Yes, speak!—that also you can do sometimes—not always.

High-Priest. Learn to be silent when an old man would be heard, and if you cannot respect my age, at least respect my misfortunes. Is the station in which I am placed that of my own free choice?—are not the nearest relations of the king priests by birth?—am I to blame because the caprice of chance destined me to the altar, to immolate turtle-doves, to draw omens from the entrails of lambs, and to interpret dreams?—Oh had you known me in my youth, you would have seen me full of ardour and energy,—more eager to brandish the sword, than to wield the knife of sacrifice!—Believe me, there are but few persons in the world placed in the situations for which they are most suited, least of all those who hold an office by descent.

Rolla. (*In a cold and constrained manner*) If I have said too much, pardon me. Overpowered as I am with rage and anguish, scarcely do I know myself.

High-Priest. Had it been possible to throw aside this dignity with which I am reproached, as one casts off a tight and uneasy garment, I had spurned it a thousand, and a thousand times; for it has occasioned me forty years of the bitterest suffering. Rolla, Rolla, I cannot endure the chilling frown upon thy countenance; the eye of contempt with which I am regarded!—Thou the only being on whom my heart still hangs!—thou only being whose affections I still wish to attract!—listen, Rolla, to my tragic story—a story nearly resembling thine own!—My sorrows, like thine, proceeded from the heart—my sorrows arose from an ill-fated passion—I too loved a Virgin of the Sun!

Rolla. How!!!

High-Priest. By virtue of my office as High-Priest, I had at all times free ingress and egress, to and from the house of the Stars. Daily did my eyes rove about among the expanding blossoms that were confined within its walls, and I was pleased with contemplating their varied charms, though this long remained a mere amusement to the eye, while the heart took no share in the glances that I cast around me. At length Zulma came, a meteor among meteors; she shone in the midst of her sisters a brilliant image of the god she served. I saw her often, and every time I beheld her, only wished more ardently to see her again—yet I continued insensible to the danger of my situation, till I was one day accidentally led into a strict examination of my heart, when I was terrified at the result. My conduct with regard to Zulma was instantly changed; I was no longer unrestrained in her presence; I scarcely dared to raise my eyes to hers; and my whole frame trembled as I approached her. I was soon convinced that her heart beat responsively to mine, since she immediately began to avoid me, as if too sensible of my meaning. I saw that the effort was painful, that love and duty were at war in her bosom, and, desirous to render the conflict less severe, I determined equally to avoid her. Many months lingered on in this miserable situation, while both endured the keenest torments of hopeless passion: our cheeks grew pale; our eyes became hollow and sunk; despair reigned in every feature; till at length Zulma's weaker frame could no longer support such complicated sorrow—she was attacked with a violent illness, and lay at the point of death; while I——Rolla, you seem affected!

Rolla. (*Holding out his hand to him with averted eyes*) Oh, how unjust have I been!—I am ashamed!—pardon me!—and—proceed, Uncle—tell me she died!

High-Priest. I hastened to her assistance—day and night I climbed the most rugged rocks, or ranged the forests, to seek medicinal herbs for her restoration. I summoned together the oldest priests in the kingdom who were celebrated for their skill in the medical science; and at length, by our unwearied exertions, the lovely Zulma was saved. She sunk in my arms overpowered with gratitude—not a word was spoken by either, we explained ourselves only by the expressive language of tears—(*He appears extremely affected*) Oh, Rolla! I am now grown old, yet see how the recollection of this scene still shakes me.

Rolla. (*Clasping his hand eagerly*) Beloved, excellent Uncle!

High-Priest. Stop till you hear the conclusion of my story!—The long-smothered flame of love now burst out with uncontroulable wildness—the voices of reason and duty were listened to no longer—passion had gained the sole ascendency in our bosoms—and——(*Rolla starts, and fixes his eyes on the High-Priest, who spreads out his arms towards him*) Rolla, you are my son!

Rolla. (*With the most eager emotion*) Old man, you mock me!

High-Priest. You are indeed my son.

Rolla. (Throws himself into the High-Priest's arms; after a few moments, he breaks from him again hastily) And my mother—is she still alive?

High-Priest. No—from above she looks down and blesses this scene! (*Rolla stands with his arms folded, his head sunk upon his bosom, and his eyes fixed upon the ground, endeavouring to restrain his tears*) Think then how my paternal heart has been tortured by your bitter revilings!—Understand why I have always clung to you with such ardent fondness!—why I have followed, you every where, and interested myself so eagerly in your fate!—The anxiety I expressed when I saw you depart to head the armies of your sovereign, is now solved!—solved equally are the transports by which I was overpowered when I beheld you return as victor.

Rolla. (Falling on his neck) Have I then ever communicated the throb of transport to any human breast?—My father!—Oh this name is so new to my tongue!—filial feelings are so new to my heart!—How often, when at the head of the army I have knelt to receive your priestly blessing, have I felt your hand tremble as it was laid upon me!—Oh, why did I not guess the cause of this tremor!—why did I not know that it was a father's blessing I knelt to receive!—My father!—my father!—why have you concealed yourself so long from your son?—why have you not sooner communicated joy to a bosom to which it has hitherto been a stranger?

High-Priest. Was it possible to trust the wildness and ardour of thy youth?

Rolla. But all is not yet clear to me. Oh then unveil the sequel of your story!—tell me—could you escape discovery?

High-Priest. What would have been impossible to another, was possible to me from my situation as High-Priest. Our hapless adventure was never known; and as soon as you were born, I sent you to the frontiers of the kingdom, among the people of Ibara, of which province my brother was governor. You were educated as his son; but as he died while you were still a child, his death furnished me with a pretence for removing you to Quito, that I, as a near relation, might take you under my protection; and, from that time, I have never ceased to pay as much attention to your education myself, as I thought I might do with safety, and without exciting suspicion. Your mother had gone to the place of rest some months before your arrival, and left me condemned for a long series of years to drag about a miserable existence.

Rolla. Miserable!—when you had a son!—I have indeed hitherto considered my existence as miserable, because I thought myself single and solitary in the world; but never shall I think it so again, now I know that I have a father living—a father who loves me, whose heart will sympathize with mine. Yes, I am reconciled to the world!—It is true, my father, that neither of us can be perfectly happy; yet a life that shall be supportable, nay in which you shall experience many hours of real enjoyment, I dare promise you. Hear what golden visions my fancy has formed:—Cora and Alonzo shall fly, we will accompany them, and I will conduct you to one who, for my sake, will be a friend to us all. There we will live,—there pass the remainder of our days quietly, contentedly, and free from cares;—and, my father, if sometimes when I witness Cora's and Alonzo's caresses, and the transports they mutually experience—if when—pierced to the heart with the idea that Alonzo's happiness might have been mine, I cannot bear to be a spectator of the scene any longer, I will make you a signal that we depart together, and leave the lovers alone; then we will retire under the shade of some neighbouring tree, and you shall soothe my cruel feelings by talking to me of my mother.

High-Priest. You do not consider, my son, that flight is impossible. Cora and Alonzo are both in chains, and both vigilantly guarded; nor will many hours elapse before sentence is passed upon them by the assembled priests. Do not then deceive yourself with vain hopes!—Cora is irretrievably lost.

Rolla. Oh do not tell me so!—I cannot bear to hear it!—she must, she must be saved!—Are you not high-priest?—the first among her judges?

High-Priest. But what can the voice of one avail against many?—against the storm of Xaira's zeal?—We may cry to the roaring winds till we are hoarse, and we cannot hinder them from tearing up the young trees by the roots.

Rolla. You will at least have done your part—God and my sword shall achieve the rest. Think, my father, when Cora shall meet your Zulma in the regions of peace, and tell her, I am a Virgin of the Sun, condemned to death because I loved———

High-Priest. No more!—All that lies within my power shall be done. I will harangue, entreat, exert every effort which the infirmities of age will permit!—Alas, the hour of judgment approaches.

Rolla. Oh fail not in your word!—Do all that you can for Cora, and remember that my life hangs upon hers—But should your endeavours prove vain, you shall find that in the mean time I have not been idle.

High-Priest. (*Taking his hand mournfully*) May we meet again, happier than we now part!—Farewell!—(*Exit*)

SCENE IV.—ROLLA, *alone. He pauses, and looks after the High-Priest—then strikes his forehead.*

Oh, my father, you know not what thoughts are brooding here!—To your powers of eloquence alone, I dare not trust a matter of this importance!—force!—force!—that is the only effectual method of persuasion.—Where can Velasquez be?—I would fain clasp him in my arms, and endeavour to communicate to his breast, an ardour equal to that which glows in mine. Yes, I will save her!—I must save her!—My mother was a Virgin of the Sun, though I must not dare to pronounce her name, lest the echoes should learn to repeat it,—to rescue Cora is a sacrifice due to her memory. Thus it is that the gods wonderfully entwine together every link in the chain of fate!—Ye powers of heaven!—you cannot be arraigned if Rolla should die poor in deeds of heroism, since you have not withheld glorious opportunities for their performance!—To give freedom to her he loves, and to present a grateful offering to his mother's memory, are objects of such magnitude, that if they did not raise a flame within this bosom, it must have been moulded from the eternal snow on the summits of the Cordilleras.

SCENE V.—*Enter* DON JUAN.

Rolla. Welcome, Velasquez!—I have waited for you here!—I have occasion for your assistance.

Juan. In what way?

Rolla. Have you sufficient magnanimity to hazard your life for a friend?

Juan. Most certainly, if it can be of any avail!

Rolla. Then give me your hand.

Juan. Take it.

Rolla. Cora and Alonzo are lost.

Juan. Alas!

Rolla. We must save them.

Juan. If it be possible.

Rolla. Only strike a bold stroke.

Juan. With all my heart!—provided it be not a criminal one.

Rolla. Criminal!—Ha!—you have touched me indeed!—Yes, I am afraid it too nearly resembles a crime!

Juan. Then seek some other person to share in the attempt.

Rolla. Yet state the question thus.—Say, which is most criminal, to institute, or to abolish, an inhuman law?

Juan. To effect the latter is an act of virtue.

Rolla. Which we will practice.

Juan. That is not in our power. This virtue can be practised by the king alone.

Rolla. Let us then counsel the king.

Juan. To that I have no objection.

Rolla. But with arms in our hands.

Juan. Such counsel were rebellion.

Rolla. What signifies a name when good is to be effected?

Juan. I am moreover much indebted to Ataliba, he has received me with hospitality, has been my benefactor.

Rolla. Your friend is in danger.

Juan. I will not commit a crime even to save *him*.

Rolla. How, if I engage my honour, that not a hair of the king's head, or of the heads of any of his servants, shall be injured,—that we will conquer by fear alone?—You know that I was once general of the army—by that army I am still beloved; for the brave fellows have not forgotten how often they triumphed under my command, nor that when we were in the field together the lowest among them was treated as my brother. To you also, Velasquez, the king has entrusted the conduct of a valiant band. On the least signal given, all who have borne arms under my standard, will assemble round me—we will ask nothing for ourselves,—sacred shall be the throne—sacred the life and property of every individual,—nothing shall be required but freedom for Cora and Alonzo.

Juan. Noble Rolla, you are blinded by love. Search your heart, you will there detect, probably for the first time, evil designs.

Rolla. I have no ears to listen to your morality. Virtue is but an empty name, if it has never been opposed by passion.

Juan. And then the stronger the opposition the more noble is the victory.

Rolla. It may be so, yet I can feel nothing but Cora's danger,—hear nothing but Cora's voice crying for help!—Look, here is Cora's grave!—Icy-hearted man, behold Cora's grave!—Yet why waste time thus ineffectually?—What interest have you in the fate of Cora?—Well then, (*He seizes Juan's hand in haste and agitation*) come with me, I will lead you to the pile prepared for your friend!—If at the sight of so dreadful an object your heart can suffer your head to reason—if on that spot I cannot inspire you with rage and anguish, equal to my own?—then farewel, I must resign you wholly to your own apathy, and fly to my mother's grave,—there as I behold the wind waving the blades of grass, and think whose form is mouldering beneath, all your precepts will in a moment be forgotten, and my soul be armed with new resolution. Come!—away! (*Exit, drawing Juan after him*)

SCENE VI.—*The Court before the Temple.* XAIRA *in conversation with other* PRIESTS.

Xaira. He stays a long time.

A Priest. Very long.

Another. The time is swiftly passing.

A Third. 'Tis now past noon.

Xaira. What could the king want with him?

A Priest. The messenger was wholly ignorant.

Another. All he knew was, that the king required to speak with the High-Priest, before sentence should be pronounced upon Cora.

Xaira. 'Tis very extraordinary.

A Priest. The messenger was in great haste.

Xaira. Probably the king wished to talk with him about the sentence,—perhaps to consult with him on the possibility of mitigating the punishment. Ah, my friends, I fear that this Inca is not eager in promoting the vengeance due to our offended gods. Didn't you remark with what reluctance he consented to Zorai's being put in irons?—with what compassion he looked upon the stranger?—nay, that he even degraded his dignity, so far as to speak to him?—His father was a very different sort of man!

A Priest. He was indeed.

Another. He never omitted attendance at any sacrifice.

A Third. And trembled whenever he entered the Temple.

Xaira. Nor ever failed in shewing due respect to our sacred office.

A Priest. Of reverencing our near intercourse with the gods.

Xaira. He cast down his eyes with awe, where his son looks up and smiles with thoughtless levity—exacted the strictest justice, where his son would shew mercy. But who are we to condemn?—who, but his tutor?—the man to whom his education was entrusted?—in short, the High-Priest. I will not say more now, this is neither the place nor the time for long harangues; however I know his principles. Take heed!—be on your guard!—

A Priest. (*Interrupting him*) He comes.

Xaira. At last.

SCENE VII.—*Enter the* HIGH-PRIEST.

Xaira. We have expected you impatiently.

High-Priest. I was summoned away to the Inca.

Xaira. Is the object of the interview a secret?

High-Priest. By no means. Ataliba requires of the judges of Cora and Alonzo, that they strictly examine whether both be equally guilty, and whether the one might not have seduced the other—might not have thrown out improper lures to lead astray the imagination.

Xaira. Well, and supposing this should appear to be the case.

High-Priest. Then he orders that the seducer only shall suffer, and that the seduced shall be released.

Xaira. Do I hear rightly?—Could the king say this, and dare the High-Priest of the Sun repeat it after him?

High-Priest. Why should he not?

Xaira. *"The transgressors of the laws shall die."*—Thus spake our god himself.

High-Priest. Did you hear the god say this?—or was it not rather spoken by the first Inca, as the ordinance of our god?

Xaira. 'Tis the same.

High-Priest. That I readily allow.—The Inca is the image of god upon earth, and the interpreter of his will; but the last Inca is equally so with the first. The severe laws, therefore, which his ancestor might find necessary to institute among a wild and uncivilized people, the descendant may be allowed to meliorate when the necessity for their enforcement no longer exists.

Xaira. (*Sarcastically*) Why then not abolish them entirely?

High-Priest. To this the king was strongly inclined. Yet he still thinks that he owes an example to the repose of his people.

Xaira. *One* example only?—And what is that to be?—He says that the guilty only shall die; but what earthly wisdom is competent to decide this question?—Will not both assert their innocence?—and will not each endeavour to throw the blame of seduction upon the other?

High-Priest. 'Tis possible.

Xaira. What then is to direct our judgment?

High-Priest. Of that hereafter. At present, duty requires that we obey the Inca's mandate. Let Cora and Alonzo be brought hither! (*Exit one of the Priests.*)

Xaira. No, I will not violate my principles, even to gratify the Inca?—Both are guilty; and whether seducing, or seduced, is a matter of total indifference. To his own face I will tell the king the same,—I will sound it in the ears of the people—and if Ataliba no longer trembles before the gods, he shall at least tremble before his own subjects.

High-Priest. Conscience is his law, and it ought equally to be ours. We are to judge Cora and Alonzo, but let us not forget that we ourselves are one day to be judged by a superior power. Now take your places.

SCENE VIII.—*The* HIGH-PRIEST *stands in the centre, with* XAIRA *at his right hand, and the rest of the Priests ranged in a semi-circle round the stage.* CORA, *and* ALONZO, *both in chains, are brought in on different sides.—Cora no longer bears the image of the sun upon her breast, nor her flame-coloured girdle.*

Cora. My Alonzo!

Alonzo. Oh God!—you also in chains!

Cora. Mourn not my fate!—I shall die with you!

Alonzo. With your murderer.

Xaira. Silence!

High-Priest. (*With mild solemnity*) We, the servants of the gods, appointed to execute their holy will, are here assembled to pass judgment upon Cora the daughter of Telasco, and Alonzo the stranger.—Oh thou, our Father above, who surveyest the whole world with one glance, diffuse thy light into our hearts!—thou hast appointed us judges over honour and shame, over life and death!—let thy wisdom then enlighten our minds that no partiality may bias them, that they may alike be free from weakness and revenge. (*He kneels, accompanied by all the other Priests.*) We swear, oh sun, to judge according to thy laws communicated by Manco-Capac!—We swear to shew mercy, if the profanation of thy temple will permit mercy to be shewn—or if strict justice be required, to exact strict justice!—We swear, finally, so to conduct ourselves, that should we be called into thy presence to-morrow, we may not be ashamed of rendering a faithful account of this awful hour!

All the Priests. We *swear* this, oh sun! (*They rise.*)

High-Priest. Cora, have you broken your vow?

Cora. I have.

High-Priest. Do you know this young man?

Cora. He is my husband.

High-Priest. Alonzo, do you know this woman?

Alonzo. She is my wife.

Xaira. You are both guilty—both must die.

High-Priest. Before we proceed to pass sentence upon you, an important duty remains to be discharged. In the name of our king, I am to announce favour to the party, who was solely the victim of seduction. Ataliba, the first-born of the sun, under whose dominion the kingdom of Quito flourishes, requires a free and ingenuous confession, which of you was the seducer, and which the seduced.

> *Cora.* It was I seduced him.   }
> > *(Both speaking together.)*
>
> *Alonzo.* It was I seduced her. }

Cora. Do not believe him, he speaks falsely.

Alonzo. Do not believe her, she would deceive you.

Cora. I alone am guilty.

Alonzo. On me must your sentence be pronounced.

Cora. Release him, he is innocent.

Alonzo. Shall the weakness of woman be punished?—No, let the man make atonement.

Cora. Oh no!—for the love of heaven! (*The High-Priest turns aside to conceal his emotions.*)

Xaira. Silence!—Who can extract the truth amid this confusion?—Let one only speak.

High-Priest. Cora begin!—Alonzo, do you remain silent.

Cora. The first time that I saw this young man was in the temple. I immediately employed every artifice to attract his attention,—I always made the longest pauses wherever he was standing, and contrived various means to continue near him—I drew aside my veil whenever I passed him, and endeavoured by expressive glances to excite his affections.

Alonzo. 'Tis false!—Her eyes were always cast downwards!

Xaira. Silence, stranger, it is not your turn to speak.

Cora. My advances inspired him with boldness—he sprang over the ruins of our sacred walls, yet scarcely was he within their circuit, when, affrighted at his own rashness, he was about to retreat without an interview. But his figure had caught my attention as I was walking at a distance—I called—I made signs to him when I ought to have fled,—intercourse with him was forbidden to me,—intercourse with me was not forbidden to him.—He stood trembling and irresolute, while I ran towards him, threw my arms round his neck, and pressed my lips to his. Still he was anxious to depart, but I detained him—he would not have returned, but I entreated him—he described to me the danger of my situation, but I refused to listen to him. On me, on me, pass sentence, ye reverend judges, it is I who have seduced.

Alonzo. Nature herself convicts you of falsehood.—Modesty is the sister of beauty—the man *declares* love, the woman only returns it. Who then can believe your story?—No, ye priests, it was I, who, when I saw her in the temple, first threw forbidden glances upon her, by which I disturbed her quiet, and ruffled the sweet serenity of her mind. It was I who disregarding the laws both of God and man, with thoughtless confidence overleaped the sacred walls, and when at sight of me she started back and would have fled, I cast myself at her feet, and holding her by her garments, forcibly detained her, to poison her mind with flattery and deceit. But why should I urge all this?—Ye judges, ye know the character of man, and must be assured, by the feelings of your own hearts, that I was the seducer. Pronounce your sentence then on me!

Cora. Recollect that he saved the Inca's life!—Spare him!—he is guiltless!

Alonzo. She raves, she knows not what she says, I alone am guilty.

Cora. Can you have a more convincing proof that I only am the criminal, when you see me wholly unconcerned and unmoved by any emotions of repentance, while the stranger is bowed down with the weight of his remorse. I glory in my guilt, and here in the presence of the gods, in the presence of all these spectators, do I embrace my husband! (*She rushes up to Alonzo, and clasps him in her arms.*) Now observe his tremor—he breaks from me, while I would still hang about him!—Can you then doubt any longer?—'Tis I,—I only am guilty.

Alonzo. Cora! Cora! Think of what you are doing!

Cora. Hear him, how he reproves, how he admonishes me!—Thus has he ever done, yet I would not listen to him, but regardless of his admonitions drew him with me into this abyss of misery.

Xaira. Shameless woman?—Tear her from him!

Cora. (*Returning to her former station*) Now pronounce sentence.

Xaira. I shudder.

High-Priest. Lead her away.

Alonzo. (*Spreading out his arms towards Cora*) Farewel!

Cora. We shall soon meet again.

Xaira. In the hour of death.

Cora. When a mightier power begins to spin the web of a more blest existence!

Xaira. Lead her away.

Alonzo. Farewel.

Cora. We part on this side of the grave with bitter tears, to meet with smiles in the realms above. (*Cora and Alonzo are guarded out on different sides.*)

Xaira. Need we any farther proof?—my voice is for death!—death to both!

High-Priest. (*Addressing the assembly with a mournful voice.*) Follow me into the temple, and let us sacrifice to the gods. Meantime, weigh well in your hearts what you have seen and heard, and then as mortals, let us proceed to pass our judgment upon mortals. (*Exeunt omnes.*)

END OF THE FOURTH ACT.

ACT V.

SCENE I.—*The Inside of the Temple of the Sun—at the Back, the Image of the Sun upon an Altar raised some Steps above the Ground. The* HIGH-PRIEST, XAIRA, *and several other* PRIESTS, *the latter of whom are employed in the Back Ground in burning Incense, and preparing the Sacrifices. The* HIGH-PRIEST *advances to the Front of the Stage with* XAIRA.

HIGH-PRIEST.

Yet one word more, Xaira, ere, by pronouncing a hasty sentence, we profane the sacred name we bear. Are we not ministers of the divine favour?

Xaira. And of the divine vengeance.

High-Priest. Vengeance!—Can we suppose that the merciful God seeks vengeance on his creatures?—No, if this principle has been encouraged to awe the vulgar, we who are initiated into the mysteries of a purer doctrine, may speak to each other without reserve.

Xaira. For what purpose?—and why at this moment?

High-Priest. Because an error committed at this moment, may draw after it an eternity of misery to us both.

Xaira. My conduct is the result of my conviction.

High-Priest. Then surely that cannot be just. God created man weak and liable to err, a truth on which your conviction should be founded. This earth is imperfect, so is every thing that lives and moves in it, and will not that God who suffers the tyger to mangle the harmless lamb, look down with forbearance on frail man when he listens to the voice of nature.

Xaira. But we men slay the tyger, and we do right,—we punish the faults of man, and we do right.

High-Priest. Yes, if by his weakness he produce disorder in the state.

Xaira. And is not that the case in the affair before us?

High-Priest. No!

Xaira. No?

High-Priest. Your own designs have been solely to avenge the gods.

Xaira. And would you then sanction the licentious conduct that must inevitably ensue, should indulgence be shewn in the present instance?

High-Priest. At the source of a clear stream, we do not think of the mud by which it may be contaminated in its course. I entreat you, let us be true to our vocation, let us resemble the god whom we serve, whose rays diffuse light and heat over all! let us acquit Cora!—It will then lie in the king's bosom to act as he shall judge right, either by confirming, or reversing, our sentence; and should it be reversed, we shall, at least, have done our duty, in shewing a disposition to clemency, while the hapless victim will breathe her last sighs in gratitude for our intended mercy.

Xaira. What would you require of me?—You speak as if the decision of this point rested upon me alone. Are not you High-Priest?—do not the duties of your office demand that you lay the case before the whole assembly of the Priests, in which I have but a single voice.

High-Priest. You know well, that in representing this affair to the assembly, I am forbidden by our laws to employ any persuasions of eloquence,—what I am to say, must be expressed in the fewest and the simplest words, and I am therefore precluded from the power of influencing the auditors. You, it is true, have only one voice, but you are the oldest of the order, next to me, and successor to the high-priesthood at my death. To you therefore all the young Priests look up, and will incline which way soever they shall see you inclined.

Xaira. This case may be rightly stated as to what concerns yourself, but it is otherwise with the Inca who has always power to grant a pardon.

High-Priest. But when has this power been exercised?—Has not every Inca, from father to son, for centuries past, uniformly confirmed the sentence of the Priests?—will Ataliba, think you, venture to deviate from the practice of his ancestors?

Xaira. No more!—It is equally inconsistent with your duty to endeavour to extort from me the sentence I shall pronounce, as with mine to listen to such entreaties. (*Turns away from him*)

High-Priest. Well then, their blood be upon thee!

Xaira. (*Coldly.*) Yes, their blood be upon me!

High-Priest. Hither ye Priests! (*The Priests assemble round him*) I already read in their gloomy countenances the sentence I am to expect! (*Aside.—After a few moments pause, in which he endeavours to assume resolution, he proceeds*) You know the criminals and the crime—we wait your decision.

Xaira. What say the laws? (*The High-Priest remains silent*) I ask you what say the laws?

High-Priest. (*After a conflict with himself, in suffocated voice*) Death.

Xaira. (*Solemnly and audibly*) The laws pronounce sentence of death upon Cora and Alonzo.

All. Death!

High-Priest. (*After a pause, and in a tone of resolution*) I cannot give my sanction to this sentence, my opinion inclines to mercy; I feel that I am myself a mortal liable to error. Search your bosoms, my brethren, prove well your hearts, and if they in a low and gentle voice whisper *mercy,*—then join with me and cry aloud mercy!—mercy!

Xaira. What say the laws?—Death to Cora and Alonzo.

All. Death!

High-Priest. Then it must be as you decide.—Oh thou unknown God, look down upon us, observe that none of this blood stains my hands!—Bring hither the unfortunate victims of your blind zeal. (*Exeunt two Priests on different sides*) The rest of you lay the sword and a fresh branch of palm upon the altar. (*They do as he directs*) Now, Xaira, follow me to the king. (*Exit, accompanied by Xaira*)

SCENE II.—CORA *and* ALONZO *are brought in on different sides. During this and the following scene, the Priests walk backwards and forwards, and are busied about the altar.* ALONZO *appears a few minutes sooner than* CORA.

Alonzo. I am struck with awe!—This temple, it is true, is only dedicated to the worship of an idol, but God is every where; even in this place, where he is adored under the image of one of his own works. This temple I have profaned!—I am brought hither as the murderer of an artless woman—as the murderer of a venerable old man who never wronged me—as the murderer of a gallant youth, one of the destined supports of his country—as one who has disturbed the peace of a liberal nation, among whom he has been received with unbounded hospitality!—Oh earth! earth! open wide, and swallow at once this monster with all his crimes!—may no grass ever grow upon his grave!—may it never be moistened with the dew of Heaven!—may no wanderer ever repose his wearied limbs upon the sods, and may they never be trodden by the innocent feet of children, in their harmless sports! (*Cora enters.*) Ah, Cora! how blest did the sight of you once make me!—how miserable does it make me now!

Cora. Alonzo, this cannot be uttered from your heart!—Have you not often declared, that if you could not live with Cora, you would die with her; and Cora has always thought the same in respect to her Alonzo. Yes, we will die together, that we may live together hereafter!

Alonzo. Oh that hereafter!—It is the haven of rest to the virtuous, but for me, an evil conscience accompanies me to the grave.

Cora. Do not think so!—we have neither of us done wrong!—we loved each other—we could not avoid loving; was it in the power of either to repress our mutual feelings? Can either of us then be criminal?—Chance, or perhaps our God himself, first brought us together—all is of his appointment, and I am resigned to my fate. Even man is kind to us, since he facilitates our union. As a Virgin of the Sun I could not have become your wife, but in death we shall be united. Resume your fortitude then, oh Alonzo!—How often have I sprung with you over the rugged stones at the breach?—Death is no more than a spring over a few rugged stones; and these once passed, we shall find love and freedom waiting to receive us on the other side.

Alonzo. Amiable creature!—thy guiltless soul can look with composure both towards the past and future.—But for me!———

Cora. How, if I can prove that you may more justly look with composure towards futurity, than Cora?—Your mother is far hence, and should she hear of you no more, will believe that your days were ended by shipwreck, sickness, or some common disaster, and this idea will console her for your loss; while her maternal fancy will see in her son nothing but what was fair and good, will frequently recur with transport to the noble actions he has already performed, and form to itself a thousand charming images of what he would have achieved had his life been longer spared. But I!—I have a father, at present, indeed, in a remote province; but who will soon learn for what offence, and in what manner, his daughter died. It is that thought alone which makes death dreadful to me!—He is so good, so venerable, and loves me so tenderly!—Were he to witness this scene, it would break his heart.

Alonzo. (*Aside*) Oh Heaven! then she knows not———

Cora. Within the last hour I fell upon my knees and prayed most fervently, that some calm and easy death might snatch my father from the world, before his daughter's fate could reach his ears. Suddenly a sweet serenity was diffused over my soul, as if the mild rays of a new sun had fallen upon me; and I hoped this was an assurance that my prayer was heard. My remaining wish is, that what I must suffer may be over quickly, lest solemn and protracted preparations should excite my rebel senses to mutiny, and shake my fortitude.

Alonzo. Oh it is the thought of what you have already endured, and must still endure, which alone oppresses my soul.

Cora. Let not my sufferings oppress you; believe me, I am resigned.

SCENE III.—*Enter* TELASCO, *with* ZORAI *in chains.*

Cora. (*Uttering a loud and piercing shriek*) Oh, I am heard!—Behold my father's spirit!—Yet his features are full of indignation!—his countenance is terrible!—Alonzo, awake me from this dream!

Alonzo. Would to God it were, indeed, only your father's shade!—but, alas! it is he himself.—Oh what an hour of horror!

Cora. (*Casting a look of awe towards Telasco*) My father!

Telasco. (*To Zorai*) Why was I brought hither at this moment?—Do not the important services which I have done my native country through so long a course of years, give me a just claim to expect some forbearance? Go and demand of the priests if I must be compelled to stay with her,—I will, meanwhile, support myself against this pillar.

Cora. (*Approaching him with trembling steps*) My father!

Telasco. (*With agony*) Save me Zorai—save me!

Zorai. (*Thrusting Cora away*) Hence serpent!—spare the old man at least in his last moments. (*Telasco turns away his face*)

Cora. (*Falling upon her knees, and clasping her hands in agony*) Brother!

Zorai. I, thy brother!—Alas, yes!—these chains speak too plainly that I am thy brother.

Cora. Father!

Telasco. (*With still averted eyes*) Who calls me by that name?—I do not know that voice!

Cora. Father!—brother!—Oh these are the only agonies of death! (*Wringing her hands*)

Telasco. (*Turning his eyes towards Cora*) Oh Zorai, my paternal feelings will not be suppressed!—It is the voice of her mother!—it is the form of her mother!—Cora!—Cora—I have passed through life with honour, and now you cover my grave with shame!—Away, away! nor hope to experience my compassion!—Do you deserve it?—Did I constrain you to devote your youth to the service of the sun?—Did I not, on the contrary, frequently admonish you to consider well what you intended? Did I not represent to you, that the world afforded many pleasures of which you were then ignorant, and which you would first learn to think desirable when their enjoyment would be criminal, and when your life would consequently be rendered miserable by the impossibility of their attainment? Even on the very last evening before your irrevocable oath was taken—(God only knows how I assumed courage for the purpose)—did I not again entreat you to reflect upon all these things while it was yet possible to retract?—Dark and gloomy then appeared the future to my soul, as the ocean on a cloudy day. Even you wept—yes, Cora, you wept; your heart was overpowered.—It was the warning voice of a guardian spirit within you; but you resisted the impulse, adhered firmly to your enthusiastic resolution, and would think of nothing but of a nearer intercourse with the gods—Behold us now standing here,— I, a poor old man with my grey hairs, mourning the honour of my house destroyed for ever;—this youth, full of energy and love for his native country, cut off even in the prime of life, guiltless himself, yet involved in your destiny;—both, both, murdered by the hand of a daughter—of a sister;— and worse than murdered, hurled to the grave with shame as their companion!—Oh that I should have lived to see this day!—Blest, blest, was thy mother's lot, that she died before the dawn of so fatal a morning! (*Cora, overpowered with her father's reproaches, sinks to the ground with a sigh; Telasco exclaims with an emotion of tenderness*) Zorai, support her!

Zorai. (*Raising up his sister, in which Alonzo makes an effort to assist him, but is thrust back by Zorai*) Hence, thou murderer of innocence!—Oh that a hero should thus sink to nothing when we behold him near!—How did I reverence this man at a distance!—how admire him when I listened to the detail of his noble actions!—I felt my young heart elevated, and wished for nothing so ardently as that I were myself in his place!—Fool that I was!—His heroism was the effect of chance, not principle; he is still but a man, and weak as the rest of mankind!—Look here, and exult at this scene, it is thy work; and thou may'st thank these chains that, even in the midst of the temple, and in the presence of our god himself, thou art not made the victim of my vengeance.

Alonzo. Did you know how my heart is tortured, how inexpressibly I love, you would be more compassionate to my sorrows!

Telasco. Say no more, my son—his fate is much more deplorable than ours: we have one treasure left, which we shall carry with us to another world, a pure conscience;—that treasure he has lost; he is poorer than ourselves.

Cora. Oh, my father, do not let me die in despair!—Can you refuse me your blessing in the hour of death! (*She falls at his feet*) I will cling round your knees, my anguish shall move you!—have pity on your kneeling daughter!—bless me, my father!—forgive me, my brother! (*Telasco and Zorai appear much affected*) See how I humble, how I twine myself about you!—Oh, my agony is inconceivable!—Have compassion upon me, or my heart will break!

Telasco. Son! son!—let us not aggravate the bitter stroke of death!—the wretched easily forgive!—Raise her up to my arms. (*Zorai raises up his sister. Telasco clasps her to his breast*) Die in peace—I forgive thee!

Cora. (*In a faint voice*) My brother!

Telasco. Yes, yes, Zorai!—no resentment!—forgive the penitent!—call her sister!

Zorai. (*Embracing her*) Unhappy—sister!

Cora. Ye gods, I thank you!—the bitterness of death is past.

Alonzo. Your hearts are softened!—Might Alonzo venture!—Zorai, you called me a weak man. Yes, I am weak; but I am not a villain!—Misery soon unites the sufferers to each other—let us not die in enmity.

Telasco. Stranger, I harbour no resentment against you!—Can I leave the world in a better state of mind, than in speaking pardon to those by whom I have been injured. Have you any parents living?

Alonzo. An aged mother.

Telasco. For her sake come hither, that I may bless thee in her place! (*He embraces him*)

Alonzo. From what a grievous burden is my heart relieved!—And you too Zorai! (*Offering him his hand*)

Zorai. Away! I admire my father's conduct; but—I cannot follow his example.

Alonzo. Not to give peace to a dying man?

Zorai. I cannot!—Would you have me dissemble reconciliation?—You are hateful to me!—leave me!—I will endeavour to subdue this bitter feeling; and should I succeed, I will reach out my hand as our last moments approach, and you will understand my meaning.

Alonzo. Accept my thanks even for this concession.—I acknowledge it to be more than I deserve. (*Cora leans against a pillar, and endeavours to recover herself*).

SCENE IV.—*Enter the* HIGH-PRIEST, XAIRA, *and several other* PRIESTS.

Xaira. The king approaches!

(*The Priests range themselves on the steps of the altar;* CORA, TELASCO, *and* ZORAI, *remain in the front of the stage on one side;* ALONZO *stands opposite to them;* ATALIBA, *attended by his suite, enters with slow and solemn steps, and with a countenance marked with deep anxiety; he kneels before the Image of the Sun, and remains for some time in an attitude of devotion, while a solemn silence is observed by all present. When his prayer is finished, he rises, and turns towards* ALONZO, *to whom he speaks hastily, and in a low voice.*)

Ataliba. Save yourself, Alonzo!—Urge that you are a foreigner, and were unacquainted with our laws and customs!—urge your services to the state, to me, to the people!—urge, in short, whatever your danger may suggest!—Your judge is your friend, let it be possible for him to shew you mercy without incurring a suspicion partiality. (*Alonzo bows silently, with a countenance expressive of ardent gratitude. Ataliba turns to Telasco*) Good old man, you are free!—He who has hazarded his life a thousand times in the service of his native country, has sacrificed it already to the gods. I dare not proceed against you!

Telasco. How, Inca!—Can you be so cruel as to deprive the aged tree of all its branches, and yet leave the trunk standing?

Ataliba. (*To Zorai*) Young man, you also are free! (*Turning to the assembly*) For it is the will of my father, that henceforward the guilty only shall suffer. (*A murmuring is heard among the priests; Ataliba casts a look of displeasure upon them, and again addresses Zorai*) Comfort your aged father, nurse him and attend upon him as long as he lives; then come to me, as to your elder brother. (*Zorai attempts to throw himself at the king's feet, who prevents him, and turns to Cora*) For you, Cora,—I can do nothing.

Cora. Oh, you have done all that I could wish!—more than I could dare to hope.

Ataliba. Your offence comes immediately within the laws, and to the laws the king himself is subject. (*He ascends to the upper step of the altar, prostrates himself once more before the Image of the Sun, and then turns towards the assembly*) High-Priest, execute your office!

High-Priest. Pardon me, good Inca!—spare my age!—my infirm state of health!—my throbbing heart!—Permit Xaira on this occasion to take my place.

Ataliba. Be it as you desire!

Xaira. (*Approaching him with solemnity*) First born of the Sun, a virgin, devoted to the gods, has broken her sacred vow!—Cora, come forwards!—A stranger who sojourns in this land is the associate of her crime!—Alonzo, come forwards!—We, the priests of the incensed gods, and servants of the Temple which has been profaned, faithful to the ordinances of thy great ancestor, have sat in judgment upon their crime, and pronounced sentence upon both.—This sentence is DEATH!!!

Ataliba. (*After a pause, addressing Cora and Alonzo*) Have you anything to say in your defence? (*Cora and Alonzo remain silent*) I ask you, Cora, and you, Alonzo, if you have any thing to urge in your defence?

Cora. Nothing.

Alonzo. Nothing.

Ataliba. How, Alonzo, have you nothing to urge in extenuation of your conduct?

Alonzo. Nothing.

Ataliba. Do not speak rashly!—I give you time for recollection!—Consider well—STRANGER!

Alonzo. I have deserved death, and submit to it willingly.

Ataliba. Once more I admonish you to consider well what you are about—a few moments longer, and it will be too late.—Oh ye assembled judges, know that I regard it as a sacred duty to grant this indulgence, since this man is a stranger, and could not be impressed with that sacred reverence for our faith, which the wisdom of our priests instils from their earliest infancy into the breast of every Peruvian. Unacquainted with our laws, he could not see with our eyes, could not know the magnitude of his transgression. Once more, Alonzo, you are at liberty to speak.—Our gods are just, reasonable, merciful!

Alonzo. I have deserved death.

Ataliba. Is that your last word?

Alonzo. My last.

Ataliba. (*Rests his elbow upon the altar, and conceals his face in his hands for some moments, then, recovering himself, proceeds*) Priests, perform your duty!

(*Two priests ascend to the altar, one on each side of the king. One takes the sword, the other the palm-branch from the altar, when, descending again, they deliver them to Xaira.*)

Xaira. (*Presenting the sword to the king*) First born of the Sun, receive from my hands the symbol of justice! (*Presenting the palm-branch*) First born of the Sun, receive from my hands the symbol of mercy!—The gods direct your judgment!

Ataliba. (*Kneels*) Oh God, thou seest how my heart is racked at this awful hour!—Grant that I may never again be compelled to the performance of so mournful a duty!—Ye shades of my forefathers, hover over me!—let me be enlightened by your wisdom, and since I exact no more than justice demands, let my soul find rest in that reflection. (*He rises—Cora, Alonzo, Telasco, and Zorai, kneel with their heads bowed down.—After a few minutes struggle with himself, the king raises the sword, and is about to speak.*)

SCENE V.—*Enter the* CHAMBERLAIN *in great haste, and with a strong impression of terror upon his countenance.*

Chamberlain. Pardon me, royal Inca, that I must be the messenger of evil tidings. The flame of insurrection rages among the people—they run wildly hither and thither about the streets—the troops assemble on all sides, crying to arms! to arms!—Drums beat, trumpets sound, weapons clash, and a forest of lances are collected together. No answer is to be obtained to a single question; all that is to be heard is the name of Rolla shouted by ten thousand voices. The troop belonging to the foreigner Velasquez, was drawn up in the meadow; I saw him run hastily from one soldier to another; and could plainly perceive by his gestures, that he entreated, threatened, expostulated, and employed every effort to restrain them within their duty, but in vain, all by turns deserted to Rolla. (*The whole assembly, except the king, manifest great consternation and alarm.*)

Ataliba. What can this mean?—Rolla, did you say, at the head of the army?— that cannot be insurrection.—Rolla's name can never be united with insurrection—this must be a mistake. Did you see him yourself?

Chamberlain. Only at a distance. The officers had made a little circle round him, he harangued them eagerly, and with a loud voice, his eyes flashed fire, which seemed to communicate to those about him, who frequently interrupted his harangue with impetuous shouts, then brandishing their swords and shaking their lances, they began to throng towards the Temple, the whole multitude following them, while I hastened on before, to prepare you for their reception.

Ataliba. (*Without changing countenance*) Well, all will soon be explained. (*He looks around*) I see terror pourtrayed on every countenance.—Why are you dismayed?—He who only studies to promote his people's happiness, has no reason to fear his people. In that conviction my heart finds repose. Let them come! (*A noise is heard behind the scenes.*)

All present cry with confusion. They come!—they are here already!

SCENE VI.—ROLLA *rushes in with a drawn sword in his right hand, a javelin in his left, and a bow and quiver at his back. He is followed by a considerable number of* OFFICERS *and* SOLDIERS.

Rolla. Be guided by me, my friends.

Xaira. A profanation of the Temple!

Rolla. You have profaned it by a sanguinary sentence.

Xaira. (*To the assembled Priests*) Avenge your gods! (*A confused murmuring is heard among them*)

Ataliba. (*To Xaira*) Silence!—(*He makes a motion with his hand, signifying that he is about to speak, when a general silence is observed. He then turns to Rolla, and addresses him*) Who are you?

Rolla. Do you not know me?

Ataliba. I had once a chieftain, who much resembled you in features—his name was Rolla, and he was a noble-minded man.—But who are you?

Rolla. No mockery Inca!—for the love of God no mockery!—Yet you may be right—I am no longer Rolla—I no longer know myself!—A storm drives me on!—a rapid stream hurries me forwards!—but have compassion upon me!—I honour you, Inca—I love and honour you truly.

Ataliba. You honour me?—Once indeed I indulged in such glorious visions, I said within myself, as long as I have Rolla for a chieftain, the monarch of Cuzco may rage, may try to seduce my provinces from their obedience, yet Rolla's heroic courage is a tree under whose shade I shall always repose in peace.

Rolla. But answer me, I entreat?—is the tree under whose shade you were reposing thus quietly, responsible to itself, if a whirlwind should come, tear it up by the roots, and throw it down upon you?

Ataliba. What whirlwind has seized upon you?—what is it you desire?—speak, and thank your former services, that you are now indulged with the liberty of speaking. I have never sufficiently rewarded your heroic achievements, I do it now, in granting this permission.

Rolla. I have only a plain story to urge in my defence, let it suffice for my vindication, if you partake more of the human, than of the divine nature!—I love to excess!—While I was still a boy, this passion stole into my heart so sweetly, so pleasantly, so devoid of all uneasiness, that I felt delight in cherishing and indulging it. Love was at that time like a day of serenity to my soul, and remained so, till the period of youth intervened, when my passion became a storm, to which all must bend,—when nothing could restrain the impetuosity of my feelings. To love and be beloved were the highest objects to which I aspired—I thought of nothing but enjoying my sweet intoxication in Cora's arms, regardless of honour or of the services due to my country, and to the noble race of our Incas, of which tree I am a branch. My good uncle sought to stem the torrent, or at least to conduct it into another channel, and sent me to serve my king in battle, trusting that the fever which burned within me, might thus in time be wholly exhausted. But vain was the hope, that in urging my steps to climb the lofty heights of honour, I might be enabled when I had gained their summit, to look down with calmness on the passion I had left below. This passion would not be shaken off—it accompanied me up the steep, and it was that alone which prompted all my heroic actions. Yes, Inca, whatever great or good I have performed in your service, is to be ascribed solely to love—it was my companion in the field of battle, and in my most adventurous moments, I thought not of my king nor of his throne, neither of the welfare of my country; I only thought of Cora— that I should become the object of Cora's admiration—You owe nothing to me, all to my love for that matchless woman, and that love you must this day pardon. I am past the days of youth indeed, but my heart remains the same, it retains all the impetuosity of my earlier years; I still cherish the lovely visions of childhood; my passion is become like a tree, the root of which is so deeply entwined with my life, that the one cannot be plucked up without destroying the other. Oh, Inca, shew that you have the feelings of a man!— extend your mercy to Cora!—on my knees I intreat for her life! (*He kneels*) Since she has called the forsaken Rolla, brother, he is become proud, yet he still condescends on his knees to beg his sister's life.

Ataliba. (*Endeavouring to conceal his emotions and preserve his dignity*) Rise!

Rolla. Mercy!

Ataliba. Rise!—lay thy arms at my feet, dismiss thy followers, and then wait silently, and submissively, the judgment of thy king.

Rolla. Mercy!—Mercy!—Uncle, Sister, aid me to entreat!—I have been so little accustomed to entreaty, that I scarcely know the form in which it should be clothed.

Ataliba. A petitioner in arms!—would you mock your sovereign?

Rolla. (*Rising up*) Oh no!—but you require impossibilities—you expect a man in a burning fever to sleep. Can Rolla behold Cora in chains, and lay down his arms?—by Heaven that cannot be!

Ataliba. I command you to deposit them at my feet.

Rolla. Pronounce her pardon Inca!—declare her absolved from her detested vow, and you shall instantly be obeyed.

Ataliba. No conditions—your arms must instantly be resigned.

Rolla. Impossible!—Come to my heart, Cora!—be my breast your shield, and let my sword hew asunder those chains!

Ataliba. Rebel, do whatever you please.—whatever the gods will permit— but know that Ataliba will not pronounce sentence till he beholds you kneeling disarmed at his feet. Never shall it be said, that you *extorted* mercy from the king. (*In a pathetic tone*) Ye people of Quito, listen to the voice of your sovereign!—I stand here at this moment, in the temple, in the presence of our God himself!—For seven years have I now reigned over you, I ask if any one can charge me during that time with a wilful injustice?—if any can, let him come forwards!—Has any one been dismissed from before my throne without assistance, where assistance could be granted?—if any has, let him come forwards!—I have conquered other countries, I have triumphed over other kings, but that is little.—When a few years ago the anger of the gods had cursed the country with unfruitfulness, I threw open the doors of my full barns, fed the hungry, and revived the sick, while many a night I lay sleepless in my own bed, because your misery oppressed my soul, and I had not power to relieve all. Ye people of Quito your present conduct is undeserved by me!—Seize that man, chain him, or I lay down my sceptre at this moment. (*A confused murmuring is heard among the crowd.*)

Rolla. (*Turning to his followers*) You seize me!—you put me in chains!—which among you will do this?—You perhaps, my old companion in battle, with whom I once shared my last morsel when famine stared us in the face?—or you, whose life I saved in the field of Tumibamba?—or you, whose son I rescued from the enemy's hands, even at the moment when the lance was pointed against his breast?—Which among you will seize me?—Speak?

High-Priest. Rolla, my adopted son, how am I bowed down by this scene. Would you see me, miserable old man, as I am, prostrate at your feet?

Rolla. Forbear!—I honour you as a father, but do not spread out your hands to the stormy winds,—it is in vain! (*The High-Priest is about to proceed in his entreaties, but Rolla prevents him impatiently*) Uncle, no more!—the lots are cast, and whatever may be the consequence I am resolved to save Cora.

Cora. (*Goes up to Rolla, embraces and kisses him*) Brother, take this kiss from your sister, and let these tears speak my gratitude for love so ardent. Your soul is truly noble,—this day, for the first time in my life, have I really known you. But one so great, so good, must be his sovereign's friend. Cora has been guilty of a crime, and would you seek to shelter her by the commission of another? Oh, what an added weight of remorse would that reflection heap upon my already overburthened conscience!—No, Rolla, do not act thus beneath yourself!—do not seek to snatch the reins from the hands of God, who assuredly directs my fate!—Suffer me to die!—I have received my father's and my brother's forgiveness; Alonzo dies with me, and I die contentedly. Our spirits shall hover around you, and will rejoice when they behold you true to your king, and devoting all your powers to the service of your country.—resolve to endure the remainder of your life without me!—it is my last request, and I know that Rolla will yield to Cora's entreaty; then will she have performed a good action at her departure from the world, and will be indebted to her brother for that grateful reflection. Yes, Rolla, I see the clouds upon your brow dispersing, I see tears start into your eyes—do not repress them,—give them free scope—they are no disgrace even to the eyes of a warrior.—And now, my brother, give me your sword, your javelin!—(*She takes his sword and javelin gently out of his hands, and lays them at Ataliba's feet*) Behold now a hero indeed!—With those tears that are trembling on his cheeks, has he washed away the stain which was beginning to tarnish his fame and virtue—now Rolla, I am indeed proud of your love!—One only effort sill remains, throw yourself at the feet of our good king—kneel to him, and let virtue remain sole victor! (*She draws him gently towards Ataliba, at whose feet she throws herself.—Rolla, after a few moments' struggle with himself, kneels by her— Cora addresses the king*) Oh sovereign of Quito, I bring you back your hero!— pardon him!—he deserves your pardon! (*She rises and returns to her former station.*) Now Inca, proceed to judgment! (*Rolla remains kneeling before the king*)

Telasco. (*Embracing Cora*) My daughter!—for as such I may now embrace thee without shame.

Ataliba. Does Rolla submit to his king?

Rolla. Entirely.

Ataliba. Your life is forfeited.

Rolla. Of that I am sensible.

Ataliba. You have my free pardon.

Rolla. (*Raising up his eyes to the king with haste and anxiety*) And Cora?

Ataliba. You are pardoned.

Rolla. (*Casting his eyes again to the ground*) Oh God!

Ataliba. Rise!

Rolla. No, let me hear the sentence upon my knees, for in pronouncing Cora's doom you pronounce mine.

Ataliba. Well then! (*He takes again into his hands the sword and palm-branch, which at the beginning of the tumult he had laid upon the altar.*)

High-Priest. (*Throwing himself suddenly at the king's feet*) Oh Inca, pardon them!

Ataliba. (*Raising him up with mildness*) Do you also ask this, my father?—have the gods manifested their will to you?

High-Priest. Mercy is the will of the gods!—Those rude times when your illustrious ancestor first established the worship of the sun are no more. Naked as the beasts of the forest, our race then lived under the open canopy of Heaven alone, while their women were considered like the dates upon the palm-tree, as fruit which every one might pluck according to his fancy. At that time they had no subsistence but what they could snatch precariously from day to day,—they were without religion, without laws, without property. Then Manco-Capac, endowed with supernatural powers, appeared among them—he built a temple to the sun, and consecrated virgins to his service, instituting at the same time the vow of chastity, because vice reigned so triumphantly throughout the kingdom, and reason was so much in its infancy, that without such a precaution, the temple on the solemn days of festival had become a theatre of debauchery. But a long series of years has changed what was then a forced obedience to the laws of order, into an inward feeling of their beauty, and where this rules, compulsive institutions are no longer necessary. Therefore, Inca, I stand here in the name of the gods, and call upon you, as the benefactor of your people, to crown all your noble deeds with a sacrifice due to reason, and through her to the gods themselves. Shrink not from the trial!—be eager to do what is right, or if any thing still be wanting to your conviction, let the supplication of an old man at least move you!—the supplication of one by whom you were educated, who loves you as his own son, who has watched with anxious care your infant slumbers, and who now asks this mercy as the recompence of all his cares! (*He takes the fillet from his head and shews his grey hair.*) Grant this request, oh Inca, for the sake of these grey hairs, become thus silvery in your service!

Ataliba. Enough!—Come forwards, Cora!—and you, Alonzo!

High-Priest. Ye gods, direct his noble heart!

(CORA *and* ALONZO *come forwards trembling.*)

Telasco. (*To Zorai*) Support me, my son,—support me!

(ATALIBA *after a solemn pause, with his right hand strikes the sword against the ground and breaks it, then with his left presents the palm-branch to* CORA.)

Ataliba. Be the law abolished, and Cora released!

(CORA *sinks down in a swoon,*—ALONZO *throws himself by her*—ROLLA *springs up and presses the king wildly to his breast.*—*The* HIGH-PRIEST *raises his hands gratefully towards Heaven*—TELASCO *supported by* ZORAI *totters towards his daughter,*—*The people shout repeatedly, crying*)

All. Long live the Inca!!! (*The Curtain falls.*)

END OF THE PLAY.